Journal of an Expedition
to the
Grand Prairies
of the
Missouri
1840

Journal of an Expedition to the Grand Prairies of the Missouri 1840

by

William Fairholme

edited by

Jack B. Tykal

THE ARTHUR H. CLARK COMPANY
Spokane, Washington
1996

Other published works of
Jack B. Tykal

Books:
Etienne Provost: Man of the Mountains. 1989.

Articles:
"Etienne Provost and the Hawken Rifle." *The Museum of the Fur Trade Quarterly,* 19: 2. (Summer 1983).
"Taos to St. Louis: The Journey of Maria Rosa Villalpando." *New Mexico Historical Review,* 65:2 (April 1990).

Contributor:
"The Pioneer Trail." *Trailing the Pioneers: A Guide to Utah's Emigrant Trails 1829–1869.* Peter H. DeLafosse, ed. 1994.
"Etienne Provost." *Utah History Encyclopedia.* Kent Powell, ed. 1994.

THE ARTHUR H. CLARK COMPANY
P.O. Box 14707
Spokane, WA 99214

LIBRARY OF CONGRESS CATALOG CARD NUMBER 96-14042
ISBN-0-87062-260-9

LIBRARY OF CONGRESS CATALOGING-IN-PUBLICATION DATA

Fairholme, William, 1819–1868.
Journal of an expedition to the grand prairies of the Missouri, 1840/ by William Fairholme; edited by Jack B. Tykal.
p. 189 cm.
Includes bibliographical references and index.
ISBN 0-87062-260-9 (alk. paper)
1. Missouri River Region—History. 2. Fairholme, William, 1819–1868—Diaries. 3. Soldiers—Great Britain—Diaries. 4. Fairholme, William, 1819–1868—Journeys—Missouri River Region. 5. Missouri River Region—Description and travel. 6. Frontier and pioneer life—Missouri River Region. 7. Indians of North America--Missouri River Region—History. 8. American bison hunting--Missouri River Region—History. I. Tykal, Jack B. II. Title.
F598.F35 1996 96-14042
978—dc20 CIP

To my daughters,
KAREN, BETSY, SUSAN AND BARBARA
who have always loved a good story

and to
WILLIAM FAIRHOLME
who tells a good one

Contents

Drawings

All illustrations courtesy of The Huntington Library, San Marino, California.

Acknowledgments

If acknowledgements are both a means of expressing appreciation for the assistance of others in the many facets of writing that go into authorship, and recognizing sources that contributed immeasurably to the volume at hand, then primary recognition, and thanks, must be given to the young Lieutenant of the British army, William Fairholme, who wrote the journal herein presented. Had he not the interest, the ability to observe, and the wit to put it all together, his journal might never have been written. More likely, it might still have been written but, without his deft pen, would lack the charm and historical insights he was able to bring to it.

The Huntington Library, San Marino, California, must be thanked not only for its foresight in obtaining the journal when it came on the market, but also for the cooperation offered, in particular by Mr. Peter Blodgett, Assistant Curator of Western Manuscripts, in the editing and preparation of this manuscript. The journal as written by Lt. Fairholme was presented to, I believe, his mother Caroline Fairholme, and remained in the Fairholme family until 1977. In that year the journal came upon the market through a Scottish bookseller, and was acquired for The Huntington with the support of a friend of the library, where it has rested since.

Included in any acknowledgements must be the National Archives of Canada, and Ms. Patricia Kennedy of its State and Military Archives, Manuscript Division. She was invaluable in not only assisting in locating data I was seeking, but also in searching out material of which I was not aware, such as the Warre manuscript. Dr. Melburn Thurman of Ste.

Genevieve, Missouri, and Mr. Craig Crease of Shawnee, Kansas, have long studied the Santa Fe Trail campsites, and are deserving of a note of appreciation for their enthusiasm for the project, and their willingness to share their expertise with me as I attempted to identify the Britisher's camp sites along the trail. And Coralee Paull, good friend and "researcher-in-residence" in St. Louis, who knows where everything is, and finds it more quickly than I, even when I am fortunate enough to be able to work in St. Louis.

Preface

The history of any society is told in all its detail through the record keeping processes of man. The records relate the courses of action, and follow the development of a society through a methodical, organized system. Most histories tell of events in matter-of-fact terms, a narrative of events and their effect to form the sequence of history. Major players are brought upon the stage to record their actions, but they are not made human.

It is in the journals and diaries of those experiencing the events recorded later as history that is found the meat on the bones of the records. The keepers of the journals are the men and women who weathered the events, and recorded what they saw, felt, and heard to reflect their intensely personal experiences at a particular time in history. They added their opinions, reactions, and insights to events that are otherwise only an entry on the long record of human circumstance, and serve to flesh out the skeleton of charted records. As one writer said, more with reference to letters, their "purpose is to reveal to us the littleness underlying great events, and to remind us that history was once real life." Certainly the same may be said for a journal, which is really a letter to oneself.

So it is with the journal of the young British army officer, Lieutenant William Fairholme. He had been at his military posting in Lower Canada for two years, and recently promoted from Ensign to Lieutenant, when the opportunity arose for him to join six brother officers in a grand adventure: a buffalo hunt to the "Grand Prairies of the Missouri." He leapt at their invitation to join the expedition, and was able to obtain five months leave-of-absence from his post in order to participate, "it being just the kind of expedition I had been long wishing to go upon."

His journal begins on that note in July 1840, and ends with his return to his post in November of that year: ". . . I had the pleasure of walking into my own room in St. Johns Barracks, having since I left it travelled upwards of 5,000 miles." The journal presented here was a gift to Caroline Fairholme in 1843, so it is obvious that it is not the field diary he undoubtedly kept during his adventure. It certainly reflects the detail of the entries that his diary must have contained, yet the depth of his reporting of events and the inclusion of his impressions and sentiments is indicative of Fairholme's capacity for reflection and is impressive in its scope.

It is the inclusion of his insights into a mid-19th century America that gives his journal its fascination for us today. Lt. Fairholme was possessed of two attributes that have made his journal an important contribution to the history of the west: he was both observant and literate. He reported the events of his journey with the eye of one who was able to discern both the foibles and magnificence of American society, and had the ability to express himself in an engaging manner. Additionally, he had some skill as a sketch-artist, and the inclusion of fourteen of his sketches along the trail adds immeasurably to both the value and interest of his journal.

His reporting is innocent of any guile or intent to misrepresent, for at one moment he praises various aspects of American society and politics, and in the next is highly critical of the American way. All in all, it is a fascinating view of America approaching the mid-point of the nineteenth century, and a detailed report of a sporting expedition to the plains of what is today western Kansas.

Historically his journal is important, for the British expedition, if it may be called that, was one of the few parties traveling the Santa Fe Trail in 1840. There were only five overland trade caravans to Santa Fe in 1840, with a total of sixty men, thirty wagons, and but fifty thousand dollars in merchandise. That was the fewest number of trading parties over the trail between 1822 and 1843. There were no American military escorts on the trail that year.[1]

Perhaps surprisingly, aside from a bit of minor thievery, the British hunters experienced no difficulties with the Indians of the Plains. They were prepared for any sort of confrontation with the Pawnee, who were the greatest potential danger to them on their journey. Fairholme's journal makes mention of the possibility of Indian dangers, and of their confidence in their ability to turn any attack. To their good fortune, they never encountered any group of Indians that either posed a threat to the party or tested their defensive capacity.

The young Lieutenant's journal (he celebrated his twenty-first birthday shortly after setting out) sweeps from the grim, as in his reporting of the prairie fire that nearly did them in, to the lighthearted, as he relates his attempts to sneak up on a prairie dog village. He is perceptive in his reporting, and adept in his writing. The combination makes a marvelous narrative of his great adventure and a valuable addition to the literature of the west for its portrayal of frontier politics and descriptions of American cities and villages in a far more bucolic age.

[1]Gregg, *Commerce of the Prairies,* 331, 2n; Sunder, "British Officers on the Santa Fe Trail," 157; R. L. Duffus, *The Santa Fe Trail,* 109; and, Beers, Henry P., "Military Protection on the Santa Fe Trail to 1843," NMHR, p. 127

Historical Introduction

They came by the hundreds in the nineteenth century, those adventuring thrill-seekers and savants, both foreign and domestic, who could not resist the magnet of the American West, deservedly spelled with capital letters in that day. It was 1843 when William Sublette, mountaineer, fur-trade partner of Jedediah Smith, supplier to the mountain trade, and St. Louis merchant, described the western adventurers to his diary. He wrote that some were:

> of the armey Some professional Gentlemen Some on the trip for pleasure Some for Health &c &c So we had doctors Lawyers botanist Bugg Ketchers Hunters & Men of nearly all professions.[2]

Sublette was commenting specifically on the make-up of the expedition led by William Drummond Stewart in that year; still, his characterization of the travelers and their reasons for venturing to the plains and mountains fits all those who went westering in the earliest years of the American West.

Of those hundreds who made the great adventure, relatively few are remembered, and fewer still made a genuine contribution to the later knowledge of the West. Those are the ones who not only kept a journal or diary, but did so with both the observer's eye and the writer's hand. A third ingredient must be a zest for the adventure undertaken, and the desire to record it all, even if only for the traveler himself, in the form of a journal.

Perhaps the earliest of these adventurers was Francois

[2]Merritt, *Baronets and Buffalo*, 37.

Marie Perrin du Lac, a young French writer who wished to visit the Upper Missouri and the Indians to be found there. He left St. Louis on May 18, 1802 as one of a party of eleven men to trade on the upper river. He related his adventures as part of his larger work, *Voyages dans les Deux Louisianes,* published in 1805.[3]

Twenty-one years later, in 1823, a young German duke, Paul Wilhelm of Württemberg, followed in those adventurous footsteps. His interest was more than casual, however, for he was a naturalist as well as a young man with a sense of adventure. The timing seemed auspicious to him: eight years had elapsed since the Treaty of Ghent, ending hostilities with Britain in the War of 1812, and peace treaties had been signed by the United States and the Indian tribes which had participated in that war on the British side. A tide of emigration was pushing against the Mississippi, and into Missouri, which had been admitted to statehood in 1821. Lastly, the many steamboats now plying the inland waters of the new nation made travel infinitely more comfortable than would have been the case just a decade previously.

As Duke Paul and many who followed him would find, the Pierre Chouteau interests in St. Louis were well qualified to assist in the planning and implementation of river adventures. But in this year of 1823, not even the mighty Chouteaus could open the way beyond the fractious Arikara Indians who lived over a thousand miles upriver from St. Louis.

Just a few weeks before the duke arrived upriver, the Arikara had attacked the 1823 fur trade expedition of William H. Ashley on its way to the Yellowstone River to resupply his partner Andrew Henry. The punitive expedition against the Indians, and its attendant activity, took most of

[3]Barry, *The Beginning of the West,* 44-45.

the summer, and it ended in what most historians regard as failure—bordering on comic opera were not the consequences so serious. Thus, it was deemed inadvisable for the party of the duke to travel beyond the Indian village. He turned around at the Missouri Fur Company post, Fort Recovery, without seeing the Upper Missouri, and returned to St. Louis.[4] Prince Paul was, however, to see the wonders of the Upper Missouri, for he returned to the west and spent most of 1829 and 1830 exploring the upper reaches of the Missouri River.

Others accepted the Chouteau courtesies in later years, properly billed for the accommodation given their ventures, and traveled the Missouri River route to the regions of the company's main river post, Fort Union, just above the juncture of the Yellowstone and Missouri rivers. Their reasons were as varied as the travelers themselves: George Catlin traveled upriver in 1832 to paint the Indians before they ceased to exist in their wild and native state. Catlin was a romantic and was in a terrible hurry to get the natives recorded forever by his brush before they were corrupted, and probably destroyed, by the white influences on their native society.

In the following year another artist, Karl Bodmer, traveled to the Upper Missouri in the employ of Maximilian, Prince of Wied. Maximilian was a German prince and naturalist, and traveled the river in his quest for information on the natural history of the region. Bodmer painted the Indians encountered at the various river posts, and the many examples of flora and fauna they found along their route. They went as far upriver as Fort McKenzie, at the junction of the Missouri and Marias rivers; however, returned downriver to spend the winter of 1833-34 at the Mandan villages, returning to St. Louis

[4]Wilhelm, *Travels in North America 1822-1824*. xx.

in 1834. Maximilian's writing added much to the knowledge of the natural history of the early west, but Bodmer's contribution in the form of his many remarkable paintings has proven to be of perhaps greater value to historians and ethnologists. Bodmer was a precise draftsman as well as an artist, and his hand captured in exquisite detail what his eye saw. There was little of the romantic in his paintings of the Indians he met, or the Missouri River scenes he portrayed. His was the craftsman's eye joined with an artistic ability that have left us with a magnificent pictorial record of the Upper Missouri country and its peoples of an earlier time.

In 1833 William Drummond Stewart undertook the first of his many trips to the mountains as an adventuring Scot. Stewart was the second son of a Scottish lord, and thus out of the running to inherit his father's estates and titles. So it was that he followed the role of many second sons and became a soldier, distinguishing himself at Waterloo, and an adventurer who traveled in Turkey before coming to that ultimate of exotic and mysterious locales, the American West. Stewart ranged over the Rocky Mountain area for five years, appearing at most of the fur trade rendezvous and gaining acceptance among the rough and tumble society of the mountaineer. Stewart made two valuable contributions to western history, albeit probably unintentionally. First, he was the author of two books, *Altowan* and *Edward Warren*. Both are romantic, quasi-autobiographies of Stewart and his adventures in the west. They do reflect events and personages of the fur trade era, and are valuable sources for that reason alone. His greater contribution, however, was to bring the Baltimore artist Alfred Jacob Miller with him to the 1837 rendezvous at the confluence of the Green River and Horse Creek, near present-day Pinedale, Wyoming. Miller, also a romantic, painted the only scenes ever made of a fur trade rendezvous. We cannot fault Miller for the sometimes romantic imagery in his works, for that was his nature, but we can unstintingly praise him for the many scenes of the west and its peoples that have enabled us today to have a greater knowledge of the fur trade. Miller was under contract to paint scenes of Stewart's great adventure which were later translated into massive oil canvases for Murthly Castle, for Stewart did, after all, inherit the estates and title following the untimely death of his brother.

John James Audubon was another naturalist who traveled the upper reaches of the Missouri River. He ventured to those areas in 1843, with Etienne Provost as his guide. His was a sizeable party of friends, naturalists, another artist, and his own taxidermist to prepare specimens for Audubon's brush. In that same year William Drummond Stewart returned to the mountains for his "Grand Adventure," to which William Sublette's earlier quote referred. Stewart traveled overland, following the old fur trader's trail to the mountains, the route later called the Oregon Trail, rather than using the river route.

Others followed; however, as the century progressed, the advent of the railroad heralded a new type of adventurer, who wanted his thrills to be accompanied by all the comforts of home. Thus, we have records of hunting expeditions led by such notables as Buffalo Bill Cody and Wild Bill Hickok, and on which servants accompanied the guests to erect the tents, lay the carpets therein, and see to the making of the beds. Ice in great (well insulated) blocks and cases of champagne eased the travail of these later adventurers to the western plains. By then, however, the great adventure of discovery was over in the west: the settlers were taking over, and the isolation and sense of exploration of an earlier era were gone. The major raison d'etre for these expeditions was the thrill of the hunt, mostly directed against the buffalo.

Yes, the British officers of Fairholme's party went to the

plains of what is now Kansas on a buffalo hunt, much as those who followed them a generation later. There were differences, however, not even considering the luxury of the later adventures. First, the Indians posed a real danger to the small number in Fairholme's party and they would have found themselves in dire straits in the face of a serious threat, despite his confidence in their ability to fend off any such danger. The larger parties of a later time faced no such threat, if for no other reason than their size. Then, too, in 1840 the west was still empty and largely unknown. The Santa Fe Trail was not a tourist road to vacationing pleasures in the southwest. Nor was it an emigrant trail. It was, in 1840, a commercial road between two population and trading centers. That anyone would travel it for purposes of pleasure was a new idea. Most of the other adventuring expeditions followed the route of the Missouri River to the lands of the American Fur Company.

The Oregon Trail did not exist in 1840, except as the fur trader's route to the mountains. The first emigrant train to follow that route to California and Oregon was a year away from starting when the British officers undertook their journey.

Who were these men who thought it fun to travel roughly two thousand miles by boat, stage, carriage, and horseback to hunt buffalo on the western plains? And why did they do it? To take up the latter question first, there has been speculation that they were sent on an intelligence-gathering mission by the British government. At least so questioned the *Arkansas State Gazette* in Little Rock on October 7, 1840.[5]

It is a reasonable question, for in 1840 the Oregon Question was far from settled, and there was unrest along the Mexican-American border. The British would certainly welcome any information that would better enable them to

[5]Quoted by Sunder in "British Army Officers on the Santa Fe Trail," 156.

assess what course of action the United States might take in the near future, and the determination with which it might act. It had long been realized that Oregon, still a territory of joint occupation between the United States and Britain, was a question yet to be decided, and that the most decisive factor would be possession.[6] The great emigration had not yet begun: that was to begin the next year with the Bidwell-Bartleson party, the first emigrant group to move over what would be called the Oregon Trail. Between 1841 and 1846 emigrants following the Oregon Trail would fill Oregon with settlers in numbers which gave little option to the British but to relinquish their claim.

Into this equation was thrown the Mexican problem, with the independence of Texas following its 1836 war with Santa Ana, and the desire of the Texans to gain annexation to the United States. The Mexican government viewed this move with suspicion, and relations between the two nations were somewhat touchy.

It would seem logical that the British government would be most interested in the situation along the Mexican border, for it would certainly be to Britain's advantage to know how tied up the United States was in its problem with Mexico, and to what degree the U.S. might become involved in a military showdown. Certainly, any military operation in the southwest would relieve pressure in the northwest, to Britain's advantage. Thus, the British might look for some indication as to what degree of force might be effective against the Americans in pushing for possession of the Oregon Territory. There is, however, no proof that "the hunting party of 1840 examined any military installations, intrigued

[6]By the Convention of 1818 the United States and Great Britain entered into an agreement for the joint occupation of the Oregon Territory for a period of ten years. This agreement was renewed at ten year intervals, until the matter was finally settled in 1846 by the Treaty of Oregon.

with the Indians, or in any way behaved as a reconnaissance party."[7] Thus, we may presume that the avowed intent of the expedition was, in truth, its sole purpose: the hunting of buffalo rather than information.

The author of this journal, William Fairholme, was born on August 8, 1819, the eldest son of George Fairholme of Greenknowe, Berwick, Scotland.[8] No information on his early life has been found, but on 19 March 1836, at the age of sixteen, he was commissioned an Ensign in the 71st Regiment, or Highland Light Infantry. He accompanied his regiment to Canada in mid-1838, and was still there when commissioned a Lieutenant on 21 February 1840, the same year in which he ventured to the plains of the American West. From the available records, it appears he had resigned his commission by the spring of 1841.[9]

In 1853 he married Grace Penelope Palliser, and with her had five daughters, one of whom was named Caroline.[10] The "Caroline" to whom the journal is dedicated, however, appears to be his mother, Caroline Elizabeth Forbes Fairholme. In the years following his military service he lived in Chapel-on-Leader, Lauder Parish, and served as Magistrate for County Berwick. While no longer in the active military, he apparently was still of the military, and he served as a Captain in the Berkshire Rifle Volunteers, which (in 1866) had a complement of 92 men. In early 1868 he fell ill, and after enduring eight days of "bronchitis and effusion in the

[7]Sunder, "British Army Officers on the Santa Fe Trail," 156.

[8]See entry of 8 August, "My 21st birthday," and Sunder, "British Officers on the Santa Fe Trail," 148n.

[9]From printed Army Lists as set forth in a letter dated 15 February 1990 from Patricia Kennedy, State and Military Archives, Manuscript Division, Public Archives of Canada, Ottawa. Also, Walford, *Walford's County Families of the United Kingdom,* 216; Fortescue, *A History of the British Army,* XI: 506; and, Rutherfurd's *The Southern Counties Register & Directory,* 528.

[10]The daughters were, for the record, Anne Gledstanes, Caroline Grace, Mary Elizabeth Eleanor, Louise Margaret, and Katherine Harriet. Rutherfurd's *The Southern Counties Register and Directory,* 528.

chest," he died at 12:30 a.m. on 20 March 1868.[11] One cannot help but wonder what part the massive doses of mercury he received during his illness in Jefferson City, Missouri, in 1840 may have played in his early death. In his journal he relates the circumstances of his illness, and that of Lt. Leicester, and while he does not state specifically that Leicester was also dosed with mercury, one may presume he was. Leicester was so ill he was unable to continue on the expedition, and returned to Canada. Both men died at an early age, Leicester in 1845 at age 32, and Fairholme in 1868 at age 48.

The senior British officer on this expedition, and its oldest participant at age 42, was Lt. Colonel William Greenwood, who was born in 1798 at Brookwood Park, Hampshire. He was commissioned an Ensign and Lieutenant in 1816, and rose to the rank of Lt. Colonel before retiring from the army in 1844, four years after this expedition. He was Lord of the Manor at Woodcote, Oxford, at the time of his death on 9 June 1872.[12] Among others on the expedition were those mentioned in the following paragraphs.

Charles William Ridley was born in 1812, and received a commission as Ensign and Lieutenant in the Grenadier Guards on 21 February 1828. Following his Canadian service he served in the Crimean War in 1857, where he commanded the Grenadier Guards. He was promoted to the rank of Major General in 1859, partly in recognition of his excellent service in the Crimea, and died on 1 February 1867.[13]

[11]Walford, *The County Families of the United Kingdom*, 351; Burke, *Burke's Genealogical and Heraldic History of the Landed Gentry*, 739; and, Register of Deaths 1868, Lauder Parish, Berwickshire, Scotland, 5.

[12]Sunder, "British Officers on the Santa Fe Trail,: 147n2, Hamilton, *The Origin and History of the First, or Grenadier Guards*, 3:480, and Burke, *A Genealogical and Heraldic History of the Landed Gentry of Great Britain.*

[13]Chicester, *The Records and Badges of Every Regiment and Corps in the British Army*, 165; Hamilton, *The Origin and History of the First, or Grenadier, Guards*, III:480; Sunder, "British Army Officers on the Santa Fe Trail," 148n.

Robert Vansittart was born 24 January 1811. On 21 September 1826 he was commissioned Ensign and Lieutenant in the Coldstream Guards, and after twenty years of military service, he retired from the Guards in 1846 with the rank of Lt. Colonel. He died on 2 May 1872.[14]

Charles Ashe Windham was the son of Admiral William Windham of Felbrigg Hall. He was born on 10 October 1810, and depending on the source consulted, was the fifth, fourth, or third son of the admiral. He received his education at the Royal Military Academy, Sandhurst, and was commissioned on 30 December 1826 as Ensign and Lieutenant in the Coldstream Guards. Following his Canadian service, he served with distinction in the Crimean War and, later, in the 1857 Sepoy rebellion in India.[15] He was elected to Parliament from his district of East Norfolk, but took leave of those responsibilities to serve in India. In 1867 he was named Commander of British Forces in North America, and died in Jacksonville, Florida, in early February 1870.[16]

Henry James Warre was but eight months older than Fairholme, having been born at the Cape of Good Hope on 12 January 1819, and was commissioned Ensign in the 54th West Norfolk Regiment on 3 February 1837. He, too, received his education at Sandhurst. Following his departure from Canada, he served in the Crimea, and later campaigned against the Maoris in New Zealand. He attained the rank of General in 1880, and retired in 1886. He died 3 April 1898.[17]

[14]Pirie-Gordon, *Burke's Genealogical and Heraldic History of the Landed Gentry*, Part 2, 2320; and Sunder, "British Army Officers on the Santa Fe Trail," 148n.

[15]Ketton-Cremer described Windham in *Felbrigg* as "impetuous and hot tempered." Windham was also apparently quite distraught at the lack of opportunity in the Crimea, and railed against the ineptitude of his superiors. It was his valorous conduct in the attack on the Redan on 8 September 1855 that caught the public eye and "converted this obscure and resentful man into a national hero." 248.

[16]*The Times*, London, 8 February 1870, p.10, Walford, *The County Families of the United Kingdom*, 1865, p. 1078, and, Ketton-Cremer, *Felbrigg*, 247-49.

[17]*The London Times*, 6 April 1898, p. 13, and Warre, *Overland to Oregon in 1845*, 137-41.

In 1845 Warre was sent from Montreal to the Oregon Territory, which at that time was still under the joint occupancy of both Britain and the United States under a treaty signed in 1818, and extended at ten year intervals thereafter.[18] Warre and his companion, Lt. Mervin Vavasour, traveled not as military men, but as gentlemen of leisure enjoying the untamed west.[19] This time the British really were seeking intelligence, and Warre and Vavasour were carrying out a secret assignment to assess the American military capability in the Oregon Territory. Their mission was to:

> carefully examine the important features of the Country in order to obtain as accurate a knowledge of it as may be requisite for the future and efficient prosecution of Military operations in it, should such operations become necessary...[20]

On arrival at Fort Vancouver in August, 1845 the two men began seven months of visiting the various settlements in the area. They submitted reports regularly but, alas for British hopes, as Warre was preparing his final report dated 16 June 1846, the issue had been settled the previous day by the signing of the Treaty of Oregon granting Oregon to the United States.[21]

The most interesting, and valuable, result of Warre's mission was the publication in 1848 of a series of sketches he had made during his journey. On a map in Warre's 1848 publication, *Sketches in North America and the Oregon Territory,* his 1845-6 route is outlined in red, and in just the barest dotted line is shown the route he followed to the buffalo grounds in 1840 with his fellow officers.

William Henry Leicester was born 4 July 1813, and commissioned an Ensign and Lieutenant in the Grenadier

---

[18]The Convention of 1818; see earlier footnote 6.

[19]Warre, *Overland to Oregon in 1845,* vi.

[20]Ibid.

[21]Ibid, x.

Guards 3 December 1830. A notice of his death states only that he "expired at his apartments in the Infantry Barracks at Windsor" on 7 November 1845 as a result of the rupture of a blood vessel five weeks previously, and a relapse just a few days before his death.[22] Here again, one must wonder if mercury poisoning in Jefferson City way back in 1840 contributed in any way to his early death.

The only American on the expedition was Robert Paterson, invited to join the Britishers in St. Louis. Paterson was born in Ireland in 1792, emigrated to the U.S. with his family in 1800, and died in Philadelphia in August 1881. First serving as a clerk in a counting house, he was later commissioned a lieutenant in the infantry in the War of 1812, and following that war, he began a successful business career, establishing several mills.

Paterson also became active in politics, working for the nomination of Andrew Jackson for the presidency in 1836, and serving as President of the Electoral College in that election. Militarily he served as a Major General of Volunteers in the Mexican War and, later, commanded the Pennsylvania Militia. During the Civil War he was the oldest commissioned Major General in the army; however, he lost favor when he failed to obey orders during the first battle of Bull Run, and was mustered out of the army when his commission expired in July of 1861.

He was one of the largest mill owners in the United States, and a very popular public speaker. At the time of his death in Philadelphia, in August of 1881, he was President of the Board of Trustees of Lafayette College.[23] Fairholme is inconsistent in spelling Paterson's name, on occasion spelling it Patterson.

---

[22] *The Times*, London, 8 November 1845, p. 5, and, *The Gentlemen's Magazine*, XXIV, December, 1845, 658.

[23] *National Cyclopaedia of American Biography*, X:250-51 and, *Appleton's Cyclcpaedia*, 673-74. Lafayette College was founded at Easton, PA, in 1826.

The journal which follows is as it was written by Lieutenant William Fairholme. The words and spelling are his. Aside from some minor deletions of unrelated material, the only changes are in punctuation, the breaking of his long narrative into paragraphs, and the division of the journal into chapter sections. The lieutenant made no such separations. He did, however, liberally sprinkle his journal with punctuatrion marks, and he wrote the journal almost as one unbroken narrative. These changes are designed to make the narrative more readable while retaining the sense of an Englishman writing about America.

Journal of an Expedition
to the
Grand Prairies
of the
Missouri
1840

St. John's River Richelieu. Canada

The Adventure Begins: Montreal to St. Louis

About the end of July 1840, being then quartered at St. Johns L.C.,[24] I had occasion to go for a few days into Montreal. While there I met Col. Greenwood, of the Grenad^{r} Gds, whom I had before known, and who told me that he had just arrived from Quebec along with a party which had been made up to go away for a few months to the Grand prairies of the Missouri for the purpose of hunting Buffalo. He proposed to me to join them, which I immediately agreed to do, if I could obtain leave of absence, it being just the kind of expedition I had been long wishing to go upon. I therefore returned to St. Johns that same evening (for they intended starting on the 1st of August, so that I had no time to lose), and having obtained 5 months leave of absence thro' the kindness of Major Denny, who in the absence of Col. Grey, was in command of the 71st, I took leave of my brother officers and returned to Montreal the next day.

I was the only officer of the Montreal or St. Johns garrison who was to accompany the Expedition, excepting [Ensign Henry James] Warre, one of Sir Richard Jackson's aide-camps. The rest of the party consisted of Col. [William] Greenwood, Captains [Charles William] Ridley & [William Henry] Leicester, Grenad^{r}. Gds., & Captains [Charles Ashe] Windham and [Robert] Vansittart, Coldsm Gds. Our plan was to go up the lakes as expeditiously as pos-

[24] L.C. refers to Lower Canada, the common term for that area at the time.

sible to Chicago at the head of Lake Michigan, and from thence to proceed down the rivers Illinois and Mississippi to St. Louis, where our further arrangements would be guided by circumstances.

Early on the morning of the 1st of August we left Montreal, and going up the American side of the St. Lawrence and Lake Ontario, we arrived on the morning of the 5th at Buffalo, a large town at the foot of Lake Erie. Finding that the steamer Buffalo would leave that evening for Chicago, we took berths on board of her, and spent the afternoon in seeing the place. The weather which was very stormy became so much worse that we did not leave till about 1 o'clock in the morning.

[6th]. On Lake Erie with a tremendous gale blowing in our teeth and a heavy sea running. The Buffalo was a very large boat, and much deeper in the water, as all these lake boats of necessity are, than the generality of American steamers. The gale increased so much that we were obliged to put in to the small town of Erie for some hours. It is a nice little place and a description of it will serve for almost all the towns on the American side of Lake Erie. Clean white houses, mostly built of wood with gardens, and rows of trees about them, are the general characteristics of these little places, and they have a quaint, cheerful appearance. One of the principal buildings is always the Hotel, where most of the unsettled part of the population as journeymen, apprentices &c. board, instead of living in lodgings as in England.

[7th]. We left Erie at 12 o'clock last night and continued coasting along the shores of the Lake, and stopping a short time at Cleveland, a flourishing little town, where they are making a Canal to communicate with the Ohio.[25] The shores of the Lake on the American side are generally well cleared

[25]The Ohio-Erie Canal linked Lake Erie on the north with the Ohio River on the south.

and cultivated & the farming seemed pretty good. At Cleveland, Greenwood bought a long-backed & crooked-legged animal [dog], which passed for a pointer and for which he paid 25 dollars, much to our amusement.

[8th]. My 21st birthday. In the middle of last night we arrived in Detroit, at the head of the lake, but we saw little or nothing of it, or of Amherstburg on the Canada side of the strait, although a most glorious moon lighted up the scene for us. A shocking occurrence had taken place just before our arrival, on board of the steamer Erie, which was lying there. The High Sheriff of the Detroit district, who had been a passenger in her, had thrown himself overboard in an unaccountable fit of panic, and was drowned: and, melancholy to relate, his daughter who was with him jumped over also, to try to save him, no one else being near at the time, and shared his fate. It was supposed that, awakening suddenly, he had imagined the ship to be on fire.

During the day we passed through Lake St. Clair, the small lake which connects Lakes Huron and Erie: it is full of fine marshes and fields of wild rice, which were swarming with waterfowl of every description. The shooting here is magnificent, both for waterfowl, snipes, and woodcocks, and more inland, on the Canada side, quail are found in great abundance. The entrance into Lake Huron is rather pretty, being through a narrow winding channel, among thickly wooded islands. Nothing can be imagined more beautiful than a fine sunset on these Lakes: I doubt if even Italy can display such richness and brilliancy of colouring.

[9th]. We were on Lake Huron the whole of this day [and] there is to me an inexpressible charm in the solitary grandeur of these upper Lakes. Rarely do you find a habitation of man on their shores, except the occasional wigwams of the Indians, whose light mysterious looking canoes may be distin-

guished gliding silently along inshore, under the shade of the dark forests, which almost everywhere extend down to the water's edge. There is a calm clearness in the atmosphere which always transports one in imagination to the Regions of the Far North. Except a few canoes, the only moving objects we beheld on Lake Huron were one or two large grey eagles hovering over some deserted looking islands covered with low stunted brush from amidst which a few dark spruce firs reared their ragged heads, charred and blackened by some former fires.

The view on approaching Michilimackinac was one of the loveliest I ever saw. The island and Mainland form a kind of strait, through which the glowing rays of the setting sun streamed with a rich golden light on the cold white walls of the Fort of Mackinaw, on the top of the cliff, under which reposed the village of Michilimackinack in comparative shade.

The only person we at first saw were a few wild looking Indians and squaws loitering about the shining gravelly beach or leaning against two or three large Nor'West canoes which were drawn up near a wigwam beautifully constructed of mats fairly worked in different colours. The houses of the village (which altogether, very much resemble a fishing village in Scotland) were dirty and dark looking, and presented a striking contrast to the pure white walls & bright green glacis of the Fort, and the beautiful yellow beach beneath them.[26]

Our arrival was an event which soon collected most of the population on the little pier. They principally consist of fishermen, this part of the lake being celebrated for the splendid trout & White fish (like a salmon) taken in it, the catching of which is almost the only occupation of the inhabitants. The

[26]A glacis is an embankment sloping gradually up to a fortification so as to expose attackers to defending gunfire.

Michilimackinac

manner of fishing is by setting lines, sometimes of a mile or more in length, with numerous hooks hung all along them (like a cross line for salmon fishing) by which means many fish are taken at a time. They lie in such deep water that nets would be utterly useless.

We remained a short time on Michilimackinac, and then proceeded through the straits till, turning due South, we entered Lake Michigan. Just at the entrance we passed the wreck of a schooner of which the masts were still standing out of the water about 20 feet, a melancholy beacon to warn others of the shoal on which she went down. We also perceived a large 3-masted ship standing to the Eastward, the only one we had seen on the Lakes.

[10th]. On arising this morning, we found ourselves lying

alongside the wharf at Manitou Island, a small island near the foot of Lake Michigan, where we had been forced to stop from the violence of the wind most of the night. By nine o'clock the gale seemed to have abated, and we quitted our little haven, but after going about 4 miles we were obliged to put back again for as soon as we got in to the open Lake the wind became as strong as ever. We spent the day in shooting hares & wild pigeons, with which the island abounded. It is quite a small place, uninhabited except by the family of the woodcutter who supplies the steamers with fuel.

[11th]. Left Manitou Island, and passing some remarkable high islands formed apparently entirely of sand and without a vestige of vegetation, we crossed the Lake and ran up along its Western Shore. In the afternoon we stopped for about an hour opposite to Milwaukie and about a mile from the town, the water becoming too shallow to allow of large vessels going nearer. A small tow boat came off with two barges of fuel, from one of which, while the wood was being taken in, we had a delicious swim in water about 100 feet deep.

Poor Windham has been suffering dreadfully during this day, and indeed has been for some days past, with a fever attack of rheumatism which will not give him a moment's rest. Milwaukie is only 35 miles from Chicago,[27] and just as we were leaving it, the Illinois steamer, which had left Buffalo 2 days after us, was appearing on the horizon astern of us, so much had we been retarded by the violence of the Wind.

[12th]. We found ourselves this morning lying alongside the wharf at Chicago, and immediately went ashore to the Lake House, a very good Hotel, where we got a capital Breakfast and good rooms. We could not resist the opportunity to go out shooting grouse (or, as they are called here,

[27]The distance from Milwaukee to Chicago is closer to 90 miles.

Manitou Island

prairie-hen), and accordingly having got hold of a sporting innkeeper, who had some good dogs, we drove out about 8 miles from the town & had some excellent shooting, killing among 5 of us (Windham and Ridley have remained behind) 18 brace. In the evening when we sat down to a supper of grouse and some broiled slices of a magnificent Lake Huron trout, I could almost have fancied myself in Scotland.

There was a box of these trout in the yard of the Hotel, containing about a dozen in ice, some of which must have weighed upwards of 40 lbs. The prairie hen is a very fine bird, nearly as large as & very much resembling the gray hen. They lie in stubbles, potatoes, or in the long prairie grass, and although they fly exactly like grouse, one would rather suppose oneself partridge shooting from the ground they are found in. Greenwood's dog, Ponto, turned out to be an excellent pointer & he gave me the reversion of him.

[13th]. Having hired an extra (or a stagecoach not otherwise running) we started about 9 o'clock this morning, not sorry to leave Chicago, which is a low, straggling, ill built, place with a perpetual miasma hanging over it. It is consequently a very unhealthy residence.

On leaving the town we entered at once upon the Prairie, and drove along over the grass as smoothly as on a good road in England.[28] The scenery of these Illinois prairies resembled that of an immense park, consisting of fine lawns & fields of grass, with large clumps of trees scattered over them and the ground is beautifully diversified in gentle undulations. Now & then you distinguish a great farm house nestling among the trees and surrounded with rich yellow fields of Indian corn, or bright green potatoe patches which form a cheerful relief to the half burnt prairie on all sides of them. The quantities of beautiful flowers and the myriads of large & most gorgeously coloured butterflies flitting about among them give a most brilliant effect to the otherwise barren looking grass.

The grouse are in such numbers that we constantly stopped to get a shot at the coveys feeding near the road, or occasionally crossing it, under the very noses of the leaders. Then there was a regular scramble, everyone trying to be out of the coach first so as not to lose time. Ponto proved invaluable for finding the wounded or dead birds in the long grass on these occasions.

[28]Sir Henry James Warre in his book *In Days of Peace and War,* noted "...If it be considered how difficult travelling was in those [earlier] days compared with our lightning speed and sybaritic ease of locomotion in these later times." 39. He also had a somewhat different opinion of the roadway for he wrote "Many a severe lump I can feel again in memory of those endured when driving from Chicago to Peoria on this very trip, when our young Yankee Jehu went for anything from an old tree-stump to a big boulderstone seldom cleared from the track." 40.

About 7 in the evening, after only breaking down once, and having left Greenwood and Vansittart a few miles behind to shoot, we arrived at Joliet, a prettily situated village, where we stopped for the night. They were here cutting a Canal which is to connect the Illinois with Lake Michigan, and which, when completed, will be a great advantage to that district; and make Chicago a place of some importance.[29] The usual want in this country, long being that of money, is retarding the operations very much. It is melancholy to see so fine a country as this is, with so many capabilities, almost entirely ruined by the wild undertakings of a few rash or knavish individuals, who with the reckless spirit of speculation peculiar to Americans, commence great works which after a time are abandoned for want of means of carrying them on, the projectors being in most cases absolutely men of straw.

We shot today along the road, 10 brace of prairie hen.

[14th]. About 9 o'clock Greenwood & Vansittart made their appearance in a pair horse waggon for which the driver demanded about 4 times his proper fare. They refused to give him so much, whereupon he obtained a warrant and took them before the Magistrate for Joliet, Mr Shoemaker. After a disgraceful scene of the most barefaced perjury on the part of 2 or 3 witnesses, this second Daniel gave the cause against them on which the boy, thinking it too good a chance to be thrown away, requested to be paid a dollar & a half for their nights lodging *which they had already paid at the house before they came away.* In vain Vansittart stormed and Greenwood expostulated: Again, the Magistrate decided against them, and to crown all, instead of the usual justice fee of 3/4 of a dollar, he made them pay him 3 1/2 dollars. So much for the

[29]The Illinois and Michigan Canal was built to connect Chicago and LaSalle, thus opening the Illinois River waterway to the Mississippi River. It was begun about 1836, and completed in 1848.

administration of Justice in the United States. And this kind of thing is not confined to the Western districts but is a general subject of complaint all over the Union. In fact it must be so where the magistrates are not raised by their situation in life above the rest of the people. In this case Mr. Shoemaker, had he decided in favor of the Britishers, could not have remained much longer at Joliet, such is the illiberal, ungenerous spirit of the American citizens. In England if such a proceeding had taken place, there would have been plenty of persons to demand fair play for the foreigners, but in the free & enlightened States of America fair play, or anything equivalent to it, is held in the most supreme contempt.

We had a beautiful drive today. The scenery was very similar to that we passed through yesterday, except perhaps in being a little more hilly & more cultivated. In the middle of the day, while the others were at dinner, Greenwood & I went into a very large stubble field near the house and found, in less than an hour, 3 coveys of at least 20 or 25 brace of birds. We had so little time that we only got about 5 brace, but I have no doubt that if we had the afternoon to ourselves, we should have found no difficulty in shooting from 40 to 50 brace in that & the adjoining fields.

About 8 o'clock we arrived at the little town of Ottawa, situated on the Illinois where, however, it is a very small stream. A handsome aqueduct for the Chicago Canal is built over the river and part of the town. The Hotel we found pretty good, and as we had shot during the day 9 brace of grouse, 2½ of quail, 2 stone curlews & a musk-rat, we had no difficulty about supper. The prairie hen is very good eating, resembling a pheasant rather than a grouse in flavour.

[15th]. Our journey today was down the Illinois through even a more beautiful country than during the last 2 days. On our right we had rich woodland and Prairie scenery, and on

our left, the river winding between some very remarkable cliffs & bluffs, some of which were quite detached from the shore. On one of these isolated bluffs a party of the Pottowattomie Indians some years ago took refuge from a War party of Iroquois, who surrounded the bluff, and encamped at its base, and the Pottowattomis, unable to escape without cutting thro' their enemies, who were too numerous for them to make such an attempt, remained on the summit, were starved to death, and their bones may still be seen whitening on the top of the cliff.[30]

We had no shooting today except one or 2 ineffectual discharges at the thousands of wild geese which were on the sandbanks in the river below us. For the last 2 miles we passed through a low bottom, completely overgrown with thistles, which were from 6 to 15 feet high & reminded me of Sir Francis Head's description of parts of the Pampas in South America. On emerging from this bottom, on to a gentle rise, we perceived on the shore of the river below us the little village of Peru, where we stopped to dine and to wait for the mail steamer in which we were to descend the Illinois. [The steamer] arriving about 4 o'clock, we embarked and proceeded in her down the river to Peoria, another small place where we arrived at 8. Having changed into another steamer which started soon afterwards, we retreated to our berths for the night.

[16th]. Continuing our voyage down the Illinois. The scenery is rather monotonous: the woods extend down to the water's edge and are very fine, the cotton wood trees and hickory in particular, often attaining a prodigious size, while the red ivy & scarlet-leafed sumach give a singularly beautiful effect to the general appearance of the forests.

[30]Site of the present Starved Rock State Park west of Ottawa, Illinois. The battle took place in 1760.

The river is very muddy, and full of sandbanks. Departed from it on each side by a narrow fringe of wood are numbers of dead, stagnant lagoons, every now & then opening into the river, and abounding in waterfowl of every description. But the effect of the slimy, sluggish water, the muddy banks of the stream covered with dead roots & branches of trees, with those disgusting looking birds, the turkey buzzards, generally perched upon them, and the marks of former floods upon the trees nearest the river, which for several feet high are covered with a dried caking of mud, is triste and melancholy in the extreme, & reminded me of descriptions of the dead, swampy rivers of Africa & South America where the demon of pestilence & yellow fever seems to have fixed his abode.

There were only wanting a few alligators to complete the resemblance, and their place was supplied by innumerable tortoises of a small size, which were basking in the hot sun on every stone or dead trunk of a tree that showed itself above water. The unbroken silence which reigns through these forests strikes one extremely: not a sound was to be heard till our steamer approached, & then the splashing of the paddles, the splitting, bursting sound of the steam (which in these high pressure boats resembles the rapid panting of a giant out of breath), the harsh screaming of little flocks of parroquets, which flew backwards and forwards as we came near them, the fluttering noise of thousands of wildfowl rising off the water, and the echoes produced by all these sounds together off the unbroken wall of forest on each side of us, formed a strange chaos of noises to which the occasional reports of our guns, as we fired at the ducks skimming past the boat, gave the appearance of a distant rattling of thunder.

Sometimes a covey of wild turkeys might be distinguished running up the banks into the forests, and now and then the bloated carcase of a dead deer, with 3 or 4 turkey buzzards and ravens hovering over it, appeared floating heavily among the debris of wood, &c on the edge of the stream.

I got a shot at a deer which, however, I fortunately missed, for just as I fired we perceived by a collar & bell round its neck that it was a tame one, probably belonging to some woodcutter near.

All these high-pressure steamboats are built on the same model. The lower part, or maindeck, is not above a foot or two from the waters edge [and] the machinery runs along 2 thirds of this to the stern. Above is built a long single room which is divided into, 1st, an open airy cabin in the forepart, with the Bar at one end, which is called Social Hall. Next to this, aft, comes the main cabin along the sides of which are gentlemen's berths, and the after division is devoted to the ladies. Outside, near the paddle boxes, are ranged in a row, 3 or 4 basins and a bucket, with which, if you want to wash, you draw the water yourself from the stream. Above them are hung a few (very few), towels, a hairbrush and comb, & perhaps a small mirror. These constitute the whole dressing apparatus of 19 out of 20 Americans, and they ridicule the idea of carrying about one's own brushes, combs &c.

Under the ladies' cabin on the maindeck, and aft of the machinery, is a cabin for the deck passengers, which has merely a few rough shelves as berths. There is no hold, or storage below, and they do not draw more than a foot or 2 of water. Dinner is laid at 2 o'clock, when the cabin passengers dine. The deck passengers feed on the remains, and the servants and crew of the ship get the leavings of the 2 first classes. The whole affair is over under 3 quarters of an hour. Each man lights his cigar at the little lamp suspended for the purpose outside the cabin door and they smoke, and drink mint juleps, gin-cocktail, &c, &c, till tea time when the same scramble is repeated. The travelling dress of an American consists almost invariably of a black coat & trowsers, & black silk waistcoat, and they are by no means remarkable for the cleanliness either of their linen or their persons.

A very few years ago one could hardly have been a couple of days in a steamer on any of the Western rivers without seeing a quarrel and bowie knives (which even now almost all Western men carry) used. The advance of civilization, however, has made this argumentum ad hominem give place to a great degree to the more harmless war of words.

None of our fellow passengers could understand our motives in leaving our comfortable homes to go on such an expedition as we were engaged in, and what puzzled them most was our disclaiming any idea of profit accruing to us therefrom.

[17th]. On going on deck this morning I found we were in the middle of the Mississippi, about 1/2 a mile below its junction with the Illinois. The shores of the left bank are high & precipitous, apparently of yellowish sandstone, and numbers of large Eagles & birds of prey were wheeling about among the broken cliffs. The water of the Mississippi is very clear, compared to that of the Illinois, and the breadth of the stream is here about a mile or so. The right bank is lower than the left, and thickly covered with wood.

In a short time we came to the confluence of the Mississippi & Missouri, and here one could distinguish the 2 rivers running alongside of each other for some distance, the one of a clear brown colour, the other resembling thin mud rather than water, till at length the turbid waters of the Missouri communicate their yellow tinge to the whole of the combined stream, which it retains until it flows into the gulph of Mexico at New Orleans, a distance of about 1200 miles from the confluence.

The high broken cliffs continue on the left bank of the river, but the right consists of an almost indescribable mass of mud, bushes, enormous trees, and all the debris brought down by the Missouri. This river is full of sand & mudbanks, and islands which are continually shifting. The banks, from the soft clayey nature of this soil, seldom retain the same appearance for a week together, and islands often make their appearance in places over which but a short time before a steamer might have passed.

Snags & sawyers form a peculiar feature in the Missouri. The former are large trunks of trees which float down the stream till they become fixed in some shallow, and one end remains protruding some distance out of the water, usually very sharp & jagged at the point. The sawyer is even more dangerous, for instead of being stationary like the snag, the upper end is moved up & down in the current about 7 or 8 inches below the surface, & is thus invisible except by the swirl of the water round it.

St. Louis is about 16 miles below the Confluence and, borne swiftly down on the broad bosom of the Missouri, we soon approached it. The smoky canopy which constantly hangs over the city is visible at some distance, and as you come within sight of the town you can distinguish tall manufactory chimneys vomiting forth black streams of smoke.

As you get nearer you perceive a line of 80 or 100 large high pressure steamers lying at the edge of the stream (there being no regular wharves), each in a diagonal direction instead of alongside. The stunning, never ceasing roar of the steam of boats coming in & departing, the hum of the bustling throng of people on the shore, the rattling of numerous drays & carts, and the loud vociferations and strange appearance of the crowds of black porters, touters of hotels, &c. who make a rush at each steamer as she takes up her berth, formed a disagreeable contrast to the silence and solitude of the prairies & forests we had for some days past been traversing.

We soon obtained a couple of carts to take our luggage up to the hotel, and in about 1/2 an hour were installed in a large 6 bedded room, the only vacant apartment in the house. [31] Having taken advantage of the nearest warm baths to undergo a most refreshing purification after our voyage, we sallied out to look about us. The town is well built, particularly the "West-End," where the houses are very handsome, with nice gardens & rows of trees about them. Being the middle of the day, when the heat at St. Louis in summer is quite overpowering, we did not see many people about, but those we did see seemed generally well dressed, and respectable looking. In the course of our walk, we paid a visit to the saddler whom Greenwood & Windham had employed when they were last here and ordered some saddles, bridles, gun-covers, &c.[32]

The saddles in general use here are made on Mexican trees of so admirable a shape that they will fit almost any horse. They are of iron wood, I think, with canvas & parchment stretched tightly over them, & slightly bound with iron, and although so light that a fullsized saddle only weighs about 4 or 5 lb., yet they will bear much more knocking about than the best English saddle.

We also went to see Mr. Kenneth McKenzie, a merchant, who was extremely civil and obliging, and offered us every assistance in his powers: and having made an arrangement with a Canadian horse-dealer to procure us horses and mules

---

[31]Warre noted that "Sleep that night (on arrival in St. Louis) was impossible; for though in the best hotel we were perforce packed five in one room; and delivered to the mercies of unmentionable small companions perfectly unremitting in their attentions, while the warmth of the weather was simply overpowering." 42. Buckingham, in *The Eastern and Western States of America,* commented, "There are 9 hotels in St. Louis, but they are among the worst we had seen in the west; even the best of them, the National Hotel, being greatly inferior to the second and third rate hotels of the Eastern cities." 126.

[32]Later in his journal Fairholme indicates it was 1838 when Greenwood and Windham were in St. Louis.

from which we should make a selection, paying him a small commission, we returned to the Hotel to tea.[33]

The object of our coming seemed perfectly well known to every one, and the people vied with each other in civility towards us. There were a good many military men boarding at the Hotel, among whom were some on the staff of General Gates, the Commander in Chief of the District. Others belonged to the 8th Regt. in garrison at the Jefferson Barracks about 8 miles down the river, and there were 2 or 3 on leave from the troops quartered up at the St. Pierre River, and the Prairie du Chien, West of Lake Michigan.

[18th]. Not being very well today, I remained almost entirely in the house. Mr. McKenzie procured for us an excellent conducteur, in fact one of the head conducteurs of the American Fur Company, by name Provost, and he promised to engage for us 7 other Canadians, & to lay in our stock of cooking utensils, provisions, &c.[34] He is to be assisted by a black fellow, named Henry, whom we have hired from his master as cook to the Expedition. He accompanied Lewis & Clark on their well known expedition to the Rocky Mountains and is slave to Clark's son.[35]

I was agreeably surprised by meeting General Patterson of Philadelphia, an old acquaintance, who is here on business, and has promised to accompany us if he can manage it.

---

[33]Kenneth McKenzie was a former (Canadian) North West Company employee and a founder of the Columbia Fur Company, an American firm which later merged with the American Fur Company. McKenzie was forced off the Upper Missouri River, where he had reigned for many years as "king of the upper river," for distilling whiskey at Fort Union. He returned to St. Louis, and entered into various private enterprises, ofttimes associated with Pierre Chouteau and the American Fur Company.

[34]Etienne Provost, a French-Canadian trapper and long-time employee of the American Fur Company. This summer he apparently had no responsibilities for the AFC.

[35]The only Negro to accompany Lewis and Clark was Clark's servant, York. James Holmberg, Curator of Manuscripts, The Filson Club, Louisville, KY, suggested that Henry could possibly be Henry Johnson, a slave in the Clark family, and apparently belonged to Clark's son, Meriwether Lewis Clark. A tenuous connection at best, but possible. Letter 2 June 1993 to Jack Tykal.

An aidecamp of General Gates called on us today, & asked us all in the General's name to spend tomorrow with him at the Jefferson Barracks, which we promised to do. We dined at the Table d'Hote of the Hotel at 3 o'clock, and had an excellent dinner. They keep 3 or 4 French cooks at the house and everything was served up in very good style. After dinner, following the example of the natives, we lounged about the door of the Hotel, smoking, & talking with the numbers of idle, well dressed men who are always to be found about an American Bar. In fact, all business in the States is carried on over a glass of mint julep, or sherry cobbler. The former is an admirable compound of mint, lemon-peel, sugar, shaved ice, and a glass or two of sherry or claret. Sherry cobbler is made merely of sherry, lemon-peel, ice & sugar.

[19th]. As I did not feel well enough to go down to Jefferson today, the others went without me and I amused myself as I best could till dinner, after which, having made acquaintance with some of the American officers, I went up to one of their rooms for an hour or two. They were all assembled there, smoking, and seemed very pleasant well informed men, great sportsmen, and with little or no Yankeeism about them. In the evening I hired a hack and took a ride for a short time, and on my return found Windham and the others just come back from Jefferson, where they had been very well treated and saw all the barracks & the 8th Regiment.

General Gates wished to send an escort of cavalry with us onto the Prairies, but as we should not in the least have known what to do with them, the offer was declined with many thanks. He promised, however, to send us some tents, which were most acceptable, and saved us one of our most expensive appointments. Nothing in fact could exceed the kindness we experienced from every one at St. Louis with whom we had anything to do.

[20th]. I went down to the stables today & after some little trouble, suited myself with a nice looking bay horse, for which I gave 70$. Just as I left the place, I found a man in the street with a most beautiful little bay mare, which I got from him for 50$. She was rather too small for me, but almost without exception the handsomest poney I ever saw. I then went to the saddlers, who had nearly finished our equipments, and sending my saddle up to the stables, I rode out my first purchase for an hour or two with Greenwood & Windham, who had bought some very nice horses. On our return from a very pleasant ride in the environs, we met Warre & Ridley, also well mounted.

During the day Provost engaged 7 Canadians for us, to whom we agreed to give 20$ a month each, & he himself to receive 80$. Vansittart and Leicester bought a light-waggon, & hired a young Canadian named Pierre for their own use, and we were glad to find that 2 large waggons which we had ordered were very nearly finished.

[21st]. On riding my horse out this morning I was very much annoyed to find him going lame. Greenwood accompanied me down to the stable, and after some discussion our contractor agreed to provide me with another. While we were talking to him, a wild looking half-breed came up mounted on a strong active roan which, as Windham and Greenwood considered him to be just the horse for Prairie work, I bought for 60$, thus changing a lame horse for a sound one and saving 10 dollars. And as Greenwood took a fancy to my little mare, & I thought she would be too light for my weight and the severe work we should have, he took her off my hands. I procured another mare in the course of the day to take me as far as Westport, where we intend to complete our studs. Greenwood also bought today a beautiful thorough bred chesnut, 4 years old & sound as possible

for 100$, and he afterwards declared that if he had him in England he would not take £150 for him.

While we were at the stables, Monsieur Soublette, a well known voyageur & trader, came in with a string of mules which had arrived a few days before from the Rocky Mountains.[36] As it was difficult to procure good mules in St. Louis at a reasonable price, we were very glad to bargain with Soublette for the pick of his at 30$ a head, and got thus 13 or 14 very good animals, in fair condition. The principal thing to be looked at in buying mules or horses to take on to the Prairie is their condition. They can hardly be too fat, and I would rather take a fat horse, although unsound, than a sound one which is not in high condition: not what we call condition in a hunter in England, but with plenty of good meat on his bones. A few days of the easy travelling of a party with waggons soon quie[t]s them down, & they will last twice as well as a horse that begins his journey in fine order.

[22nd]. All our saddlery was finished today and the waggons were also ready. In the afternoon Windham & I, finding ourselves completely equipped, resolved to ride out to the Prairie House, an inn about 3 miles from the town. The grand point in any expedition with Canadians is to get away, no matter how short a distance, so as you make a beginning. The night before starting is spent in taking leave of their friends, and they are seldom perfectly sober when the hour for moving arrives but, once off & their business fairly begun, they are the best of all travellers and give no trouble.

[36]William Sublette who, with Jedediah Smith and David Jackson, bought out William H. Ashley's interests in the fur trade in 1826 to form the partnership of Smith, Jackson and Sublette. He later became a major supplier of the trappers in the mountains through his partnership with Robert Campbell, as Sublette and Campbell. In partnership with Campbell he operated a mercantile store in St. Louis.

The Adventure Continues St. Louis to Westport

[22nd-cont'd].We therefore quitted St. Louis about 4 o'clock leaving the rest of the party to follow next day, and after a pretty ride of 4 miles arrived at the Prairie House, just as a tremendous thunder storm set in. We found no one in the stables and cleaned & fed our horses ourselves, literally by the glare of the lightning, for it was not till we had nearly finished that a drawling ostler made his appearance with a lanthorn.[37]

We took supper with 3 or 4 traders, who were going up the banks of the Missouri with dry goods, and from whom we gleaned a little information about the roads. The only things they seemed to be afraid of were the musquitoes, which on some part of the route are a serious evil to people travelling with horses.

[23rd]. Finding that I still required a few little things, I rode back early to St. Louis, meeting Ridley on the way, who was coming out to join us. I found the rest of the party nearly ready to start, but there seemed to be some doubt as to the strength of the waggons, and there had been no bridles provided for the men. The latter were soon procured, and not withstanding the ominous prophecies of some Yankees about our waggons (for they wanted us to buy 2 or 3 that they had brought down to the Hotel on speculation), we managed to get away at last, and amid the adieux and good wishes of a

[37] Ostler is a variation of hostler, or stableman.

respectable crowd that had collected to see us off, we quitted St. Louis, and passing a little way off from the Prairie house were joined by Windham and Ridley close to Monsieur Soublette's farm. We made a very fair show for the party now consisted of 3 waggons, (2 pair mule, & one single mule) 13 mules, 19 or 20 horses, 7 of ourselves, and 10 men.

The country we passed through was well wooded and very pretty; and about 5 in the evening we halted at a small village where we got a beautiful meadow to encamp in.[38] It was a small haugh along a little clear stream, and being well fenced in, was an excellent place to turn the animals loose in.[39] They seemed to enjoy it very much, rolling about among the rich grass, or tearing & scampering round & round it for some time after we came in. It is amusing to observe the contempt the horses have for the mules, who on their part, never fail to resent it with a scream & kick whenever one of the horses comes near them.

This being our first camp we were very assiduous in cutting wood, helping Henry to cook, &c., all of which was very troublesome to him & the Canadians, who consoled themselves by the recollection that we should not give them much of our labour after the first day or two. I was much surprised by putting up near the camp a rabbit exactly the same as the English rabbit, which I did not know was found in this Country; it certainly is not known in Canada.

[24th]. We started early this morning, after some trouble in

[38]With respect to their own dress, Warre wrote "Our hunters' costume was considered somewhat unique. We had donned Canadian home-made shooting-jackets with numerous and enormous pockets, very wide-brimmed straw hats, light breeches and long jack-boots, a double-barrelled rifle, and pair of pistols in holsters apiece, with, lastly, high Spanish saddles cut down to as English a trim as was possible.

Though quite satisfied with ourselves as to our appearance, we were taken at our first halting-place for a wild beast show, and were accordingly hailed with due delight by the inhabitants of the little town we stopped at." 42.

[39]A haugh in Old English was "a corner of land." A later, Scot's, meaning is "a low-lying meadow by the side of a river."

catching the horses, &we had to pay the proprietor of the farm for some damage done by one or 2 of them to a fence & a field of Indian corn which they had got into. Before leaving, however, we each chose one of the men as a servant. The best of the whole of them, Jean Baptiste Tabaud by name, came to offer himself to me, giving as a reason that he had formerly known my old roan horse in the Rocky Mountains. I afterward found that almost all the men recognized him by the name of Cendre[40] (from his colour) as having been one of the most celebrated Buffalo horses in that district, and Provost told me he had several times been sold at from 300 to 500 dollars.

As we proceeded the air echoed with snatches of Canadian songs, shouted forth by our men, who seemed a very good set of fellows, merry civil & obedient. Henry the cook, who was a bit of a wag in his way, gave us much amusement. He had taken unto himself a vicious devil of a mule which he named Josephine, and was constantly scampering up & down the cavalcade, sometimes mounted, sometimes driving Josephine before him. Whenever we came to a house, which was but rarely, however, he managed to procure a bargain in the shape of eggs, butter, watermelons, &c.

The whole of this day's journey was thro' an open oak forest with a good deal of gentle hill & dale. The wood was quite open without any undercover, & the trees were beginning to take the rich hues of Autumn so peculiar to America.

Altogether it was pretty scenery, but after riding through it for 15 or 16 miles it became rather monotonous, and we could not get a drop of water, all the little rills & streams being dried up.

We generally rode in front while the waggons, each driven by one man, kept together, followed by the rest of the men mounted on the other mules, & leading the spare horses,

---

[40]Atkins, Beryl T. et al, *Collins-Robert French-English, English French Dictionary*, Ontario, 1983, defines "cendre" as blond, or ash-colored.

making the woods resound with their noise & laughter. And each man with his pipe in his mouth, for a Canadian is nothing without his pipe. We stopped for the night near a cottage at the foot of a steep hill, where we hoped to find water, but were disappointed, and we had to take all the animals nearly a mile into the wood to a dirty pond. However, we got an enclosure for them, and plenty of Indian corn husks to feed them on.

[25th]. We were glad to get away early this morning for a drove of pigs, attracted by our fire & the smell of cooking, meandered through the camp the whole night and prevented us getting much sleep. In the boundless oak forests along the Missouri, vast droves of these animals (many of them of a breed nearly approaching to the wild boar) are turned out to feed on the acorns, and on the approach of winter they are exceedingly fat, and are then killed and frozen. In this state they are sent away in large quantities & form a great portion of the food of the inhabitants in the Western states. During the time they are in the woods they become so wild that when wanted they are obliged to be shot and the forests become tainted with them like a boar park in Germany.

Our route today was precisely similar in point of scenery to yesterdays. We saw no game of any description, principally because we did not give ourselves the trouble of looking for it, for the woods teem with deer, bears, wild turkeys, racoons, opossums, &c., especially toward the Missouri, parallel to which our road lay at the average distance of about 6 or 7 miles.

Our horses & mules were all very good, except my last purchase which was a regular Rosinante,[41] but as I had only given 30$ for her & only intended to take her to Westport, I was quite satisfied. We halted at a very pretty valley, where there

[41]Rosinante, according to *Webster's Third New International Dictionary*, was Don Quixote's bony horse, and has come to mean a broken-down nag.

was a good deal of cultivation, & in which the luxuriance of the woods & creepers among the trees was quite astonishing. A clear, trouty looking stream ran through it, & on the border of this, under some enormous cotton-wood trees near a small farm house, we pitched our tents. The owner of the farm, a very fat old widow, was very civil and permitted us to shoot as many chickens as we required for supper [and] providing us with an enclosure for our animals.

Just as we had finished supper, the sky became suddenly overcast and a loud, crashing peal of thunder reverberated thro' the valley accompanied, not preceded, by a blinding flare of lightning which seemed to blaze up like a vast furnace on all sides of us, and in a few minutes such a torrent of rain came down as if the clouds had fallen bodily on our devoted heads. A general rush was made for the farm house, which we soon filled, & remained there an hour or two, during which the storm raged with a violence utterly incredible to one who has not witnessed such a hurricane. After that it seemed to abate and Windham, Leicester & I went into one of the tents where with a bottle of sherry, & some cigars, we were very merry till the storm increasing drove us again into the house.

[26th]. The storm continued the whole night but, in the morning, the rain ceasing, the sun soon made his appearance, and nature was laid out to dry, an example which we followed by spreading out our tents and bedding &c. to the sun, which by midday had become overpoweringly hot.

As it was impossible to think of moving today, Windham & Vansittart went into the woods to look for game, and in the afternoon returned with a fine young wild turkey, the only one they had seen, & the first we had shot. It resembled a common tame turkey in every respect except that there was a fine gloss on the feathers, resembling that on the tail & neck of a peacock.

[27th]. At an early hour this morning we quitted the "Slough of Despond," as we named this place,[42] and ascending a steep hill about 1/2 mile from it we came to a scattered village perched on the very crest of the Mountain, from which we had a very extended view. On our left we looked down upon the richly wooded and half cultivated valley we had just left. On our right, just below us, flowed the river Gasconade, while in front, behind and all around the valley, was an amphitheatre of high hills clothed with the most luxuriant forests, with all the varied tints of the Fall just beginning to show themselves.

Descending to the stream, we were ferried across in two large scows and continued our journey up the left bank. No words can give any idea of the rank luxuriance of the vegetation in this low valley. Enormous forest trees were laced and netted together by a profusion of creepers, among which the peavine, which resembles the hop-plant, was the most conspicuous, running far up their vast stems and forming, high up above our heads, the most beautiful natural arches & tracery and hanging in the most graceful festoons in every direction.

We continued in this beautiful valley during the greater part of the day, till at length, leaving it to the left, we turned over some high ground, and after traversing an open forest for 2 or 3 miles, we descended into another pretty little valley, near the upper end of which we turned off the road into a narrow path through a thicket of hazel bushes and, in a short time, reached an open space on the margin of a small, clear stream, where we encamped under some fine trees. We found an enclosure near in which we put the animals, and then enjoyed a most delicious bathe in the stream which, although the water scarcely reached our middles, we found most

[42]The "Slough of Despond" is taken from Bunyan's *Pilgrim's Progress,* used in the sense of deep, hopeless dejection or discouragement.

refreshing and invigorating after our dusty journey. From the quantities of filberts we found here, we christened this place "Filbert Camp."

[28th]. Windham and Vansittart went out this morning to look for turkies, but did not kill any, though Windham heard some near him; and as soon as they returned, "Up Camp" was the word, and getting back into the road, we renewed our journey. A great part of the track today resembled a dry watercourse rather than a road, & some of the hills being very steep, were a very severe pull for the mules in the waggons.[43]

The interminable oak forests continued as before, and late in the evening, which was becoming very dark & stormy looking, we turned off the road about 1/2 a mile to the left, and arrived at a farmhouse where we stopped for the night. We did not encamp, as the farmer very civilly gave us a good barn to sleep in, and it was very fortunate we had such a refuge, for about two hours after we put in a storm came on which rivalled that at the "Slough of Despond" & lasted the whole night.

[29th]. In spite of our barn we got very wet, and were obliged to remain here to dry our bedding &c. till 11 o'clock. Warre was forced to leave behind a very handsome Buffalo robe, which even in that short time began to show evident symptoms of being tennanted by certain maggots.

We found that one of the waggon axles was out of order, but as there was no blacksmith within 12 miles, we had nothing for it but to push on. It held out till we were close to the smith's, and as he said it would take some time to repair it, we encamped near his shop which, with 2 or 3 other houses, formed the nucleus of some future settlement. We spent the day in walking about the woods in search of game but, owing

[43]At this point the party was on the Boonslick Road which paralleled the Missouri River from St. Charles to Franklin, Missouri.

probably to the numbers of pigs scattered all through them, we were unsuccessful. I was a little startled during my walk by seeing what I at first took for a bear, but it proved to be a large black porker, who took a long look at me, & then made off into the bush.

[30th]. I was so unwell this morning that I found myself unable to ride, and took advantage of Vansittart's offer of his little waggon, but the extreme roughness of the road made it a matter of nearly equal difficulty to keep my seat & to drive.

We went along some high, sharp ridges covered with low, stunted coppice,[44] and every now & then had a fine view of the country over toward the Missouri. The woods seemed to abound with deer, & some of us got shots at 3 which passed near the road, but they did not fell any. The only chance I had was at an enormous golden eagle which came hovering over my waggon, and I let fly at him with a pistol, with no better success than the others at the deer.

About 6 in the evening we reached the village of Burtonville, a small place where we put up at the Inn and got a good stable for all the horses & mules. This place is 2 days journey from Jefferson city and about 8 miles from the Missouri: we had now come nearly 150 miles from St. Louis.

[31st]. The first few miles of our road today were through an open, partly cultivated country, but we soon entered the oak forests again, which indeed extend nearly the whole way up the Missouri from St. Louis to Westport, a distance of 350 miles.[45]

Preceding the rest of the party, I kept with my waggon close behind the Jefferson stage coach which, from the exceedingly bad state of the road, could not go faster than I did. Indeed I only wondered how it got on at all, for the road was merely a watercourse covered with large boulders &

[44]A coppice is a thicket of small trees or shrubs.

[45]By today's roadways, closer to 250 miles.

Osage Ferry

loose gravel, while every now & then the wheel would sink down about a foot in a deep rut, or I would be nearly hoisted out by going over the stump of a tree.

After traveling over a good deal of hilly ground, we arrived at the top of a tremendous place which appeared to be a precipice, and I supposed the road turned away along the top. Not a bit of it: to my astonishment I perceived the stage commence descending, the heavy unwieldy coach swinging from side to side as if it would roll over at every moment into the river which flowed at the foot of the hill. I followed, and after about a quarter of a mile of such a road as I hope I shall never have to drive down again, I came to a low flat valley, & in half an hour more I emerged from the thick forests into an open meadow on the banks of the Osage river and close to the ferry house. The stage drove down at once onto a large flat scow moored near the shore and three or 4 men in long black coats & trowsers, & very shiny new hats, proceeded to row her across the stream.

I resolved to wait for the rest of my party and let the mare pick a few mouthfulls of grass while I took a sketch of the scene. It was really very pretty. The ferry house was nearly on a point formed by the junction of the Osage and the small stream I had followed down from the hill, and had some fine cottonwood trees growing about it. In front was the smaller river, about 60 yards wide, with a fine high wooded bank opposite, on which were 2 or 3 houses To the right flowed the smooth but rapid Osage, here about 120 yards in width, the banks on the other side thickly wooded down to the water's edge.

Just as I had finished my sketch the party arrived, having by a miracle gotten the waggons down the precipice without injury, and at the same time the ferryboat returned and we learnt from the men that it was owing to the late very heavy rains that we found the roads in such a state.

The party being so large, & it being Sunday, they at first demurred a good deal about taking us over, but after a little trouble and by setting our own men to work at a small scow that lay near the other, we were all transported in safety to the other side, having only to deplore the loss of a large dog belonging to Windham, whose melancholy howling we heard all night long from our camp, which as the evening was too dark to admit of our making it by the river side, we formed at a large farm about 1 1/2 miles beyond the stream. It was by far the nicest establishment I had seen in any part of the States, & the old farmer & his dame made us sit down to an excellent supper while their daughter, a pretty girl of 18 or 19, waited upon us, assisted by several clean, merry-looking slaves who seemed much amused with us for we were probably the first Britishers they had ever seen.

We had much fun in the evening with Provost & our hearty old host, whose brother, a wandering trader in the Rocky Mountains, was well known to Provost and most of our men, and the former accounted to us several wild adventures they had together with the Pawnees & Blackfeet Indians.

[Sept. 1st]. I awoke this morning exceedingly unwell having, I believe, rolled out of my bedclothes on to the grass outside the tent which, from a heavy dew that fell all night, was quite wet. I could not eat anything at breakfast so, taking leave of our kind hosts, I started in my waggon before the rest of the party and after a pretty drive of about 3 hours I arrived at Jefferson City on the Missouri about 12 o'clock.

It is a straggling place but the site is pretty, the houses being scattered over the sides & bottom of a little valley down to the edge of the Missouri, here about 200 or 250 yards across. They were building a remarkably handsome Courthouse, which stands in an imposing situation about halfway up the valley, and which it is said will be the finest building in the United States. I had not much inclination to make any remarks on the scenery then, however, for I felt extremely ill and drove up at once to the best inn in the place where I was soon joined by the rest of the party. Poor Leicester being also very much indisposed, He & I agreed to remain here till we were more fit to proceed, & accordingly the others took leave of us after dinner, having agreed to wait for us up at Westport before going on to the Prairies.[46]

[46]Warre's account covers the overland travel of the group from Jefferson City to Westport, which Fairholme was unable to do because of his illness. On 4 September Warre noted that "Our day was enlivened by seeing a regiment of militia at drill. It was the most absurd scene. Their multifarious costumes and the dégagé air with which the men obeyed their commanding officers were extremely droll. We dared not laugh, as they soon found out who we were, and 'guessed they'd whip the Britishers...'" 45.

In the evening I was obliged to take to my bed, and sent for a doctor who, giving me mercury in quantities that would have astonished an English M.D., told me that I had a severe attack of fever & ague. He had the prudent kindness to inform me at the same time that 3 men had died of it within the last week at that house.

[7th]. During all the past week I was nearly insensible & was given over twice. Poor Leicester finding himself getting worse every day, went away back to St. Louis yesterday, having most kindly delayed his departure 2 days on my account Indeed, but for him & a dear little Englishwoman who, with her husband, was boarding at the Hotel, I do not think I should have lived, for the people of the house took scarcely any trouble about me and little groups of the townspeople used to assemble in my room at all hours of the day to stare at me.[47]

In short, what with my uncomfortable state at the Inn, my fears of losing my party, and my being, after I had paid my bill at the house, without a farthing of money (having to give even the doctor a bill on a man at Independence to whom McKenzie had recommended us), I got quite desperate and on this evening had myself carried down to a steamer which happened to arrive from St. Louis on her way to Westport.

The Captain was very civil and gave me a comfortable berth and a nice lad to attend on me, which latter was very necessary for I was so weak that I could not stand up without assistance, and being salivated by the quantity of mercury I had taken, could eat nothing but mashed apples & port wine negus.

[47]Warre commented on the illness of both Leicester and Fairholme: "Leicester could not resist the temptation, having had enough of western camping-life. He said good-bye and went back to civilization. Though very sorry to lose so excellent a companion, we saw his health was not up to the hard work. Poor Fairholme would have done wisely to have returned with him: being down with fever which lasted several weeks and reduced him sadly." 44.

[10th]. For the last 2 or 3 days we were steaming up the Missouri. Being confined to my berth, I saw but little of the scenery, but it appeared to be the same kind the whole way. The river itself is the most peculiar feature: the steamer was continually winding & twisting about among the enormous snags & sawyers and masses of trees & bushes laced together with which the course of this extraordinary stream is constantly interrupted, while in some places the whirlpools, eddies, currents, rapids & sandbanks (covered with thousands of Canada geese) together with the tremendous violence of the waters, form a spectacle the grandeur of which I have never seen at all approached except in the rapids above Niagara. Very often the whole power of the engines was barely sufficient to resist the impetuous fury of the stream and every now & then we would drop down, till, gathering new way, & "vires acquireus anudo," we would slowly work past the contested point, which was usually some immense snag which formed a "hell of waters" boiling & hissing around it. We saw few settlements, the villages generally being 2 or 3 miles back from the river with roads leading down to small wharves on the waterside called "landings," at which goods & passengers are left or picked up by the passing steamers.

The numbers of boats that go up this immense stream is astonishing considering the difficulties of the navigation & the comparatively wild state of the country, & they all seem to load well, both with goods & passengers. This, however, is only during the summer & autumn for the river is rendered impassable in the winter by the quantities of ice, although from the great strength of the current there are not many places where it is entirely frozen over.

About 8 in the evening the steamer stopped at a small wharf, which I was glad to find was the Westport Landing, and accordingly disembarked.[48] There was only one house there, belonging to a family of Germans. The good man finding that I was too weak to go on to Westport that night, offered me a bed in his house & at my request drove into Westport to see if he could obtain any account of my party. I took some tea & then lay down on my bed which, with 2 or 3 others, was in a large room at the top of the house.

Presently my hosts' two daughters, fat, laughing little frauleins, came up to dress for a ball which they told me was going on at a farm house near. They did not seem to trouble themselves in the least at my presence, but chattered & laughed away while dressing until, just as they were ready, a spruce little Frenchman in an antiquated suit of clothes, brought in, I should think, with the first settlers of Louisiana, came in his waggon to escort them to the ball, as their father had gone on my errand to Westport. He returned not long after they had gone, and having received from him the joyful intelligence that the party would reach Westport tomorrow, I soon composed myself to sleep.

[11th]. At 8 o'clock this morning a waggon & pair arrived from Westport for me, and after a very pretty drive of 4 miles thro' fine forests, I alighted into the outstretched arms of Mynheer Vogel, an honest little Dutchman who had been very kind to Greenwood & Windham on their last expedition here, & who hearing of my arrival, had come to request me to make use of his house.[49]

I was very pleased to accept his offer & being quite exhausted with my drive, lay down on a bed where I slept till

[48]Westport Landing was located at the foot of today's Grand Avenue in Kansas City, Missouri.

[49]Lewis Vogel, a well-known early resident of Westport who was a grocer and "beer maker." A "grocer," in the parlance of the 1840's was a saloonkeeper, contrasted to a greengrocer, who sold foodstuffs. Etienne Provost was undoubtedly right at home with Herr Vogel, for he operated an inn and "grocery" in St. Louis when not otherwise occupied by his employer, the American Fur Company.

my host's bride, whom he had only married a day or two [earlier], came to ask me to take some dinner.

Just as we began 2 or 3 horsemen rode up to the door & I had the pleasure of seeing Windham, Greenwood & Warre walk into the room, very much surprised to find me there.[50] They had preceded the rest of the party, and joined us at dinner. Every thing had been going on well except that my old mare, having become knocked up, they exchanged for a very nice Indian Poney. At Independence they were joined by General Patterson, who had resolved to accompany the Expedition, and soon after dinner he & Vansittart & Ridley came in. It is impossible to describe my delight at finding myself once more with my friends, after all my troubles & fears of their having gone on, and one must have been in the forlorn kind of situation I was at Jefferson, without money & too weak to do anything for myself, to enter into my feelings.

The men & waggons were sent on to a farm about 2 miles beyond Westport, where they formed a camp, while we remained in the village as we had many things to do before starting onto the Prairie.[51] At Independence they had bought a quantity of Indian corn to take with us for the horses, to carry which a large box-waggon has been hired, with a negro driver. We spent a very merry Evening with Herr Vogel, as he was well provided with Beer (a great luxury in that country), champagne, &c.

The village of Westport is prettily situated, surrounded with fine woods. The inhabitants seem mostly Dutch & Germans, and Indians of the Konza, Delaware, and

---

[50]Warre: "Much to our surprise, Fairholme had followed by steamer, and, passing Independence, had landed at Westport. He was dreadfully weak and could barely move. We did all we could to persuade him to return, but he would not hear of this, so he rejoined the party." 49.

[51]Westport was then, and still is, located just about one mile east of the Kansas/Missouri state line, which in 1840 was the western border of the United States. This line was established by survey in 1823 as running south from the confluence of the Kansas and Missouri rivers. Letter of Craig Crease, 30 July 1993.

Shawnee tribes, whose villages are scattered along the frontier, are constantly to be seen in the place. They come in to exchange their furs, skins &c. for such goods as they require from the stores. They are what are called Missionary Indians, being for the most part Christians, and having Missionaries living with them, and appear to be a much finer race than the Canadian & other Northern tribes, with good features, & tall slim figures. We generally sees them mounted on stout galloways[52] of an active hardy appearance, which their character does not belie and, as they cantered about the streets dressed in bright coloured blankets and handkerchiefs, they formed a conspicuous characteristic of a border village.

I slept at Vogels on one bed while he & his wife occupied another, with a child in a cradle-bed between us. Windham & Greenwood, wrapt in their buffalo robes, stretched themselves on the floor. The others went to a little inn.

[12th]. We were all busily occupied today in buying horses, getting spare horse-shoes made, & other preparations. Patterson made up his stud to 5. Windham bought a powerful, wellbred chesnut horse, and the others also got another horse or two each. I procured a very nice chesnut for 60$.

We also engaged a very nice German boy, son of a carpenter who was doing some jobs for us, as assistant Cook & servant of all work. He was a nice sharp lad named Fritz. All the party except myself proceeded in the evening to the Camp but, as the ox-waggon had not arrived, and some of my horseshoes & other things were not ready, I remained at Vogel's. I had become a little better during the last 2 days and was able to smoke a pipe, a great comfort to me as I was not able to eat any thing solid.

[52]A galoway (galloway in the journal) is a breed of small hardy horses of former times, originating in Galoway, Scotland. A second definition, applicable here, is any large pony or small horse.

Commencement of a City in W. America

[13th]. Rode out in the forenoon to the camp, and being caught in a heavy storm, had to take refuge with the man I had bought my chesnut from. On arriving at the camp, I found it in a regular swamp & the tents & everything drenched with the rain. I joined them at dinner & afterwards, the storm coming on with renewed fury, I took advantage of the owner of the field, Mr. Parker's, offers, & went to his house close by for the night.[53]

The roads became so broken up by the torrents of rain that we thought is advisable to send some of the mules down to assist the oxen with the waggon, which was on its way, and on

[53]Craig Crease, by letter dated 30 July 1993, identified Parker as Joseph Parks, a leader of the Shawnee Indians. His home was on the Santa Fe Trail out of Westport, and just barely across the line in Kansas. Fairholme later notes that Mrs "Parker" was a Shawnee woman; Parks was one-quarter Shawnee.

their return the camp was broken up and they moved off 4 miles into the Prairie, leaving me to join them next morning.

At supper our numbers in the farmhouse were increased by the arrival of 2 men who had come with a train of mules that morning from Santa Fe, a Spanish settlement just under the Rocky Mountains. They told me that they had seen no Indians this time, but while going out in the Spring they were surprised by a party of Pawnees & lost upwards of 100 mules. They said we should not be likely to find Buffalo in any numbers within about 300 miles, which is rather further than we expected.

In the evening Mr. Parker read prayers and all the household joined in singing some hymns, which they performed very well. Mrs. Parker was a Shawnee squaw, and her mother & sister were living with them: they were all very pleasing looking with soft, musical voices & fine, mild black eyes.

The constant glare of the lightning in my bedroom left me awake most of the night; it was like a house on fire near at hand.

The Adventure On The Prairies

[14th]. Early this morning while engaged at a breakfast worthy of Scotland, I was joined by Vansittart, who had ridden back to get some things he had forgotten at Westport and who told me to ride on slowly towards the camp, & that he would overtake me on his return. Accordingly, after breakfast I mounted old Cendre, and taking leave of civilisation for some time to come (& with much more anticipation of pleasure than any feeling of regret), I commenced my journey into the Prairies of the Far West, or as they are called par excellence, the Grand Prairies.

The boundary line between the United States & the Indian territory is well defined & so jealous is the American government of any interference with the Indians that a fine of 1000$ is inflicted on any person going on to the Prairies without a passport, which necessary documents had been provided for us by the Indian Agent at Westport.[54] This excellent regulation is, I believe, principally for the purpose of checking the introduction of arms & spiritous liquors amongst the Indians, both of which articles were formerly smuggled in in large quantities, to the great detriment of the tribes. It has been invariably found that the imposition and

[54]A letter from Joshua Pilcher, Superintendent of Indian Affairs to Major W.R. Cummins, Indian Agent at Westport, dated August 25, 1840, noted the departure of the party from St. Louis and advised the Agent that the penalties of the law would apply should the party fail to seek the necessary license; however, it was to be granted "as a matter of course, specifying their objective to be recreation or Amusement," if they did apply. U.S. Superintendancy of Indian Affairs, vol. 7. Kansas State Historical Society.

rascality practiced by the traders (a class of men abandoned to every vice & depravity) has not only caused the degeneration of the Indians, but also inspired them with distrust and hatred of the white men, and the care the American government now take that such practices may cease is a creditable exception to their general treatment of the natives.

For the first 4 miles of my journey the track was plain enough, till I arrived at the farm belonging to Missionaries where the encampment had been formed last night.[55] Here I found the Negro in charge of the ox-waggon who had been detained from following the party by 2 of his oxen having got loose during the night, & which having been sent after, he was now waiting for. He directed me which way to go & I followed what seemed the trail of the party. For some miles I passed through a very pretty, undulating country with a great deal of fine wood, amid which were many nice looking small farms belonging to the Indians, generally prettily situated among the trees.

I then emerged into the open prairie and proceeding for 2 or 3 hours without seeing any signs of the party, I began to suspect I had lost my way. To add to my discomfiture, I had forgotten to put my compass in my pocket, and there were so many different paths leading in all directions towards the different Indian villages along the frontier, and intersecting each other continually, that it was almost in vain trying to keep to any one, and I became completely puzzled. My weakness, too, made it a painful exertion to sit my horse & I was just beginning to think of retracing my steps (if I could) to the Missionary farm when, joyful sight, I perceived a figure

[55]This is probably the Friend's (Quaker) Shawnee Mission, which was about four miles from the home of Joseph Parks. There were several Indian mission organizations; established in 1839, and just west of Park's property, was the Shawnee Methodist Mission, which is still in existence today. The Friends Mission no longer exists: the site is (today) the Shawnee Mission High School. There was also a Baptist Shawnee Mission. Craig Crease, 4 August 1993.

far off on a distant swell of the prairie. Immediately striking off across the Prairie toward it, I had the additional pleasure in about 20 minutes of discovering it to be Vansittart. He also had lost his way, and as companionship even in misfortune carries with it a certain degree of consolation, I was not at all inclined to regret the mistake which by so singular a chance had, among so many tracks, caused him to follow almost the same I had taken. After a short consultation we proceeded for about 3 miles further along the track I had been following & then being quite convinced that we were wrong, we turned back toward Westport.

Presently we met a large, straggling party of Indians, men, women & children, who were returning from a great field preaching, or Camp Meeting, which had been held for some days past near Westport. We found from them that the Santa Fe trail lay quite to the North West of us & while Van took directions from them about the road, I had time to take a glance at the party.

The scene was really very picturesque. The Prairie was here quite bare of trees & rolled away on each side of us in long sloping undulations, while far in the blue distance could be discerned the vast forests bordering the Missouri & Konzas Rivers. The Indians were about 30 in number, all mounted on their wild looking ponies & dressed in gaudy colored blankets, handkerchiefs &c., & their wild gestures & black gleaming eyes were in perfect keeping with their savage attire. The men were all armed with rifles & long knives, but they were perfectly civil and most of them insisted on shaking hands with us when we parted from them.

We immediately took a short cut across the prairie toward the Santa Fe trail, and by the directions they had given us & the help of Vansittart's compass, we chose our line so well that about an hour after sunset we perceived a grove of trees in a bottom below us with some horses pasturing about it, and after a few moments of anxious suspense & hard galloping, we recognized, with feelings of delight which may be easily conceived, some of the horses as our own. In a short time our weary steeds were rolling in the high grass of the bottom, and we were seated with our friends round the fire. They had dined, but Henry soon warmed us up something & I was by no means sorry to roll myself up for the night in my blanket in the tent instead of sleeping, as but for Vansittart's arrival & good pilotage I should probably have done, on the open prairie under the canopy of heaven which, in the state I was, would perhaps have been my death warrant.

This camp was named Round Grove, & was a pretty grove of wood with a small creek running thro' it, & with good pasture.[56]

Vansittart & I must have ridden at least 40 or 50 miles today, instead of about 19.

[15th]. The morning was raw & wet, and we did not break up the camp till the afternoon when it became a little clearer. Our party now consisted of:

Col. Greenwood	4 horses	Warre	3 horses
----- Ridley	4 -----	Fairholme	3 -----
-----Windham	5 -----	Paterson	5 -----
-----Vansittart	6 -----		

Mons: Provost, conducteur & 2 of his nephews. *Jean B. Tabau* & 3 other Canadians. *Pierre,* Vansittart's servant: *An American,* Patterson's servant; *Henry,* the cook & *Fritz,* assist [cook], and *Julius,* the negro who drove the ox-waggon. 14

[56]Located just south of present-day Olathe, Kansas. Craig Crease in "The Lone Elm and Elm Grove Case: A Study in Mistaken Identity," and by letter dated 30 July 1993, identifies two very separate and distinct sites in this area of the Santa Fe Trail: Round Grove campground, which was the same as Lone Elm campground, and which was on the Santa Fe Trail out of Independence, and the Elm Grove campground, which was about 2½ miles northwest of Lone Elm, and on the branch of the trail coming from Westport. Based on Fairholme's description. Mr. Crease believes the party was on the Elm Grove site.

Round Grove

mules, 8 oxen, 3 dogs, 1 large waggon 2 pairmule [wagon], covered over with striped canvas, and Vansittart's little wagon.

In all, 19 men, 44 horses & mules, 8 oxen, 3 dogs, & 4 waggons. Our route lay across a continued rolling prairie, with Indian trails crossing it occasionally, and every now & then as we came upon high ground we obtained an extended view around us. To our right lay the thick belt of wood bordering the Konzas River, which joins the Missouri a short distance above Westport. Far beyond that, and looking like a blue haze on the horizon as it appeared occasionally between the distant swells of the Prairie, were the forests of the Missouri, and in our rear we could just distinguish those that surround Westport.

The dry clear air of the Prairies, the consciousness of actually entering those very scenes I had read of with such delight in Cooper & Washington Irving's Works, and the feeling of independence naturally produced by cantering along on a good horse over such a boundless extent of open country, free from the trammels of civilised life gave me (& I believe all of us) an elasticity of spirits which even the enervating effects of my illness could not altogether repress. Having no money, nor need of it for the time, was also another cause of lightness of feeling which, we all remarked as quite delightful. About 6 o'clock we arrived at a small stream with a few trees growing about it where we encamped, and which is known to the voyageurs under the name of Elm Grove.[57]

[16th]. This morning while the men were collecting the horses before starting, one of Ridley's, by accident, got loose and after snuffing the morning air for a moment, turned around and gallopped off toward Westport. Tabaud, being the most active of the men, was despatched after him, mounted on another of Ridley's horses, & taking with him 2 day's provisions in case the runaway should return to Westport which, as he had been bought there, was not improbable, and we proceeded on our journey.

After going 5 or 6 miles we halted for breakfast at a place called Black Jack Grove, so named from the wood there being principally the Black Jack Oak.[58] The country was

[57]Near present-day Gardner and the Lanesfield school. Warre noted their first campground was about fourteen miles from Westport at "a small creek called Round Grove....[The next day] In the evening we continued west about four miles to Elm Grove, so-called, I suppose, from there being one elm-tree at a spring of very bad water." 50. Craig Crease identified this site as being the campground at Bull Creek crossing, and within a mile of the parting of the Santa Fe and Oregon trails; the Santa Fe Trail continuing southwest, and the Oregon Trail branching to the northwest.

[58]Warre differs on the distance covered. "After going about fourteen miles, we remained to breakfast...we then proceeded on the trail formed by the traders between Westport and Santa Fe in Mexico." This is the only mention made, or recognition given, of the fact the party was following the Santa Fe Trail.

prettier than yesterday as we had struck the outermost edge of the forests bordering the Konzas River, and the spot where we lighted our fires was in the middle of a copse of low brushwood, into which we turned the horses and mules to feed, and having to dry our blankets &c., we hung them all about the bushes, so that the scene was highly picturesque from the gay colours of the clothes & the numbers of animals moving about the bushes, & the gipsy appearance of our waggons and tents. To the right the deep, wooded valley of the Konzas, with its sides broken by many gulleys & ravines, and the boundless prairie in front of, and behind, us formed a good finish to the picture. We waited here for a short time after breakfast in hopes of being rejoined by Tabaud, but as we saw no symptoms of him, we resumed our march. Our direction was generally about S.S.W., and during the whole of this day we continued skirting the edge of the Black Jack Grove, which extends for many miles Westward.

We occasionally got beautiful views down the Valley of the Konzas as every now & then we mounted some little eminence.

Most of us kept dispersed along the line of march, looking for Prairie hens, of which we shot a few, but as Greenwood was beginning to complain of illness (which he attributed to Mynheer Vogel's strong ale, but which seemed to me rather to have a feverish tendency) and did not feel much inclined any more than myself to ride as fast as the others, we kept each other company most of the day, riding quietly in front. Late in the evening we reached our camping ground on the side of a deep gulley in Black Jack Grove.[59]

There was but little water & not very much wood, but the pasture was good, and we managed pretty well. Great numbers of these gulleys and ravines intersect the steep banks of

[59]Near present-day Baldwin City, Kansas. Undated letter, Marc Simmons to Jack Tykal [1990].

the Konzas, and altho' at this season dry, during the heavy rains in Spring and later in the Autumn, they become the beds of rapid streams, which all run towards the North & Northwest.

Our proceedings on arriving at the Camping ground were generally as follows: The waggons were first placed in such positions as to be convertible, if necessary, into a defence, the animals were then turned out as near the camp as the pasture would admit, tethered with lassos of rope about 20 feet long, which were strongly pegged down to the ground at such distances as to allow of the beasts feeding without interfering with, or entangling, each other.

The fires were lit by some of the party; others pitched the tents, unpacked the provisions and cooking utensils, fetched water, or cut a supply of firewood. In short, every one had something to do, either for himself or others. By the time dinner was ready all our private arrangements of bedding &c. in the tents were completed, and after dinner, stretched around the ample fire, we smoked & chatted till by degrees it was abandoned for the tents, each one dropping off from the circle as he felt inclined for repose.

At first starting from Westport we had made an equal division of all the provisions with the voyageurs, who took charge of their own share, while Henry looked after ours, so that there was no interfering with each other in the cuisine department except when either party sent a deputation to request a loan of a pot or pan or such small articles as pepper, salt, mustard, &c.

Our two tents were always pitched near our own fire, close to which also was placed Vansittart's little waggon, which contained most of the cooking things. The Canadians had their own fire, near which was their own tent. We divided the men into 3 watches during the night, one man being on watch at a time: indeed it was part of our agreement with them that *we* should not keep watch, and we paid them a few dollars a month more on that account for the usual custom is for *every one* in a party to take his turn at watching.

Old Provost, being conducteur, was in our mess which, thanks to Henry, was an excellent one. We generally had a large bowl of capital soup, meat roast & boiled, generally some game, plenty of potatoes and onions, biscuits, &c. & plenty of tea & coffee. In the evening we moistened our pipes with *hot stopping* or brandy & water, usually without sugar.

Our costumes were various, red shirts perhaps predominating in our attire, & we had plenty of guns, pistols & ammunition and a large supply of spare knives &c. Paterson brought with him a lance, with which he intended to spear the Buffalo as they do hogs in India, but he never used it.

We liked our men more & more every day, particularly Tabaud & Henry. The latter, though occasionally sulky, was an excellent fellow, as strong as a horse, always active and doing something, and an admirable cook. Fritz proved of great use in assisting him or in peeling potatoes, fetching water & lighted sticks for our pipes, &c. Paterson's man was also an exceedingly willing, hardworking, fellow.

We had all been prejudiced against him, as being an American, and also from his previous character having been rather doubtful. He had lived all his life among the Rocky Mountains, & a year or two ago was in the service of the present Sir William Stuart of Murthly, who has lived a great deal about these prairies.[60]

On one occasion Stewart lost a horse and, in the anger of

[60]Sir William Drummond Stewart, a Scotsman and second son, who adventured in the west from 1833 to 1838, attending all the fur trade rendezvous during those years. He visited the U.S. again in 1843 for one final "grand adventure" to the mountains. This 1843 adventure is well covered by Matt Field, who was one of the adventurers, in his book, *Prairie & Mountain Sketches* (University of Oklahoma Press, 1957).

the moment, was heard to say that he would give 500 dollars to recover him, or to get hold of the man who had stolen him. Our friend slipped out of the camp on hearing this and in a few hours returned with the horse. It afterwards turned out that the animal had only been taken in a prank by a lad of the party who went out on him to kill some Buffalo. On his return toward the camp he was met by this man, who engaged him in a conversation and, while the boy was off his guard, he seized hold of his gun, placed the muzzle to his head & shot him dead, and then took the horse back into the camp and claimed the reward as if nothing had happened. However, with us nothing could be more satisfactory than his conduct, although from what we had heard of him we kept an eye to him as he was just the sort of fellow to go off some fine night with some of our best horses.[61]

[17th]. Our route this day took us away from the course of the Konzas River, which here turned Northward while the trail took a S. Westerly direction. Paterson and Windham rode a long way in front to look for a camping ground as there was no wood to be seen during the whole journey.

About 6 in the evening we perceived Paterson far on ahead making signs to us to advance (we having halted for the signal). We gladly obeyed, but on joining him we were much annoyed by finding that he had made a mistake, which was rectified by Windham, who came up soon after and made us retrace our steps about 3 miles to a small grove of Beechwood a little to the right of us, where we encamped. The place was like an old quarry with a little green haugh and very few trees large enough to make our fires, but there was no other wood

[61]The man's name was Mark Head, or Markhead as Stewart and Ruxton wrote it. The event Fairholme relates occurred in 1834, and the story is told in Leroy Hafen's *Mountain Men and the Fur Trade,* vol. 1:289 as well as by Mae Reed Porter in her biography of Stewart, *Scotsman in Buckskin.* The incident was also told by Ruxton and Alfred Jacob Miller. Mark Head was "a specimen of the devil-may-care mountain man," and a somewhat legendary figure. He was killed during the Taos Rebellion in January, 1847.

Little Neosho Creek

within 7 or 8 miles of us, and as the pasture was good, we were satisfied.[62]

The ox waggon was not able to keep up with us this day, and being afraid that it might pass the place where we had turned off the trail, we were obliged to send one of the men there to guide the driver to the camp, but he returned after waiting 2 or 3 hours without seeing anything of it. The whole of this day's march was tedious and dreary beyond description and the weather was dark and louring [lowering] with a drizzling rain at night.

[62]At about this time in his account Warre wrote "We have discovered a remarkably pleasant incident. Not one of our men, not even the 'guide,' have ever been [over] this trail before. Windham and Greenwood went nearly the same course about two years ago, but they do not seem to know much about it; so we must resort to our luck to find wood and water." 52.

[19th]. We were much gratified this morning by the arrival of Tabaud leading Ridley's truant horse, and driving before him 2 of the oxen. He had followed the horse all the way to Westport and last night overtook the ox waggon about 4 miles back. Finding some of the oxen very much knocked up, he & the driver camped together there and came on early this morning, and he had left the waggon at the trail, waiting our coming. He was very hungry, having eaten nothing since yesterday morning, poor fellow, and we waited a little to give him time to get some breakfast.

About 9 o'clock we started, and without any occurrence worthy of mention, arrived about 5 in the evening at the Little Neosho Creek, where we camped in a very nice spot on the border of the stream, which was clear and full of fish, but as in most of these small prairie creeks, they were only catfish, which are not good eating.[63] We also found a few ducks, and numbers of parroquets* were constantly flying over our heads in little flocks, making a great screaming as if indignant at our intrusion. Our bivouac was in the middle of the remains of an old Indian encampment of which, however, only a few sticks remained standing showing where the lodges had been.

[20th]. The same wild, desolate prairie country stretching away in long, undulating swells in every direction as far as the eye could reach, without a single object on which it could rest, except occasionally a far distant clump or fringe of trees, looking like a wreath of blue haze. One is apt to be much

---

[63]The party was not in the Neosho River drainage at this point in their journey, but in that of the Osage drainage. Dr. Thurman writes: "Fairholme was clearly aware...that the camp was on one of the southward flowing drainages....As there are few decent sized southward flowing creeks actually crossing the (Santa Fe) trail before before 110 Mile Creek...I am convinced that Fairholme's 'Little Neosho' was 110 Mile Creek." Letter 7 July 1990. This would place the party in the vicinity of present-day Scranton, Kansas.

*Fairholme's note: Psittacus Carolinensis—(Wilson). Ed. note: the Carolina Parakeet is extinct today.

Great Neosho Creek

deceived as to distance on the prairies. The air is very clear, and there being so few objects to guide the sight, every thing appears much nearer than it really is, except wood, which always struck me as seeming further than in reality.

When you begin to be a little tired with perhaps a tedious days' ride, it is very tantalizing, after mounting long successive wells of land, to find that you still have to go over others, which seem interminable, instead of descending into the green, fresh-looking and wooded haugh you hoped for.

This is peculiarly the case when in search of water. You see in the hollows between the rising ground low, marshy looking spots covered with long, rushy herbage of a greener appearance than the rest of the scorched & withered prairie grass and hasten down, your horse as eager to be there as yourself, but when you reach the desired spot, you find it dry and hard like the rest with occasionally a slight crusting of salt on the part where the water had lain, a bitter disappointment both for man and beast. Then what a delight to find, perhaps in the next valley, a clear, bright spring gushing forth from among the long rank grass & reeds which usually overgrow such places. Instantly a general rush takes place among the horses & mules who are soon burying their muzzles in the sparkling water and cropping the sweet young grass round the edges of the spring.

After a long days' journey we were delighted to perceive, on rounding the side of a higher elevation than usual, a fine thick wood about a mile below us in a rather pretty valley. In a short time we were encamped on the main branch of the Neosho River, on a beautiful flat green at the edge of the grove, where we found quantities of excellent mushrooms which were by no means thrown away on us.[64]

Windham walked into the wood with his gun and almost immediately shot a brace of wild ducks. Had it not been too late in the day, we might have got plenty as there seemed to be numbers of them about the creek.

After dinner Old Provost & Henry related to us some stirring incidents of Indian warfare, of which they had seen a good deal, having lived a great part of their lives among the Indians and in the Rocky Mountains. Provost on many occasions had very narrow escapes and was wounded in several places. Henry had more than once owed his preservation to his colour, for the Indians have a superstitious feeling about killing a black man, and also with regard to people with red hair, as Henry archly remarked to Warre in the course of conversation.

[64]Dr. Thurman is of the opinion that this camp was most likely at the Dragoon Creek crossing, some three miles west of today's Burlingame, Kansas. Letter of 7 July 1990. Other options that would fit the mileage figures given by Fairholme are either Switzler's Creek, to the east, or Soldier Creek to the west of the Dragoon Creek crossing.

112-Mile Creek

The American government is in the habit of sending to certain tribes persons in different capacities, as blacksmiths, carpenters, &c, to teach their crafts to the Indians, and Henry had been for 4 or 5 years attached to a tribe of Delawares as a farrier & blacksmith, during which time he had some very wild & interesting adventures, which he recounted to us with much spirit and which, had I the pen of Cooper or Washington Irving, I should like to have noted down.[65]

[21st]. We travelled today about 18 miles to a place called

[65]James Holmberg, Curator of Manuscripts of The Filson Club, Louisville, KY, suggested in a letter that it was not unusual for a slave owner to contract a slave's services out to the government, much as he might do to another individual, and pocket the government's payment.

112 Mile Creek from its being reckoned that distance from Westport.[66]

We let the horses run loose today, for the first time, as we were now far enough from the settlements to do so without any fear of their returning if left to themselves. When horses once get fairly on to the open Prairie nothing will induce them to separate from the main body, and if by any accident they lose sight of their companions, they evince every symptom of excessive fear, snorting and trembling in every joint. Nor are they pacified until they once more get within sight of them.

Today they seemed to enjoy their freedom very much, gallopping about along the line of march in small detached bands but always keeping within half a mile or so of the waggons. My old Cendre and a wicked little Indian mare of Greenwood's seemed to take the lead in all the mischievous pranks. Every now & then they would assemble in a body behind the mules (who generally kept soberly together near the waggons) and suddenly swept past them at full speed, screaming , kicking & snorting at their quieter fellow travellers.

In the evening we came to a fine creek running through a thick grove, which we passed through and encamped about 200 yards on the other side where we found good pasture. Some of us immediately went out to look for game, of whom I was one, but an hour's walking through such thick, tangled brakes as I had to force my way through shut me up com-

[66]Sunder in his "British Army Officers on the Santa Fe Trail" noted that Fairholme was likely in error in calling the site 112 Mile Creek. Overland parties frequently stopped at 110 Mile Creek, and Sunder believed that was probably the party's campsite for the night. It is near Scranton, Kansas. Dr. Thurman disagrees, believing that the 112 Mile Creek designation actually referred to 142 Mile Creek, or Elk Creek. That site was 142 miles west of Ft. Osage, the point of origin of the 1825 trail survey, and is north of presentday Allen, Kansas (Letter of 7 July 1990). Craig Crease states both 110 Mile Creek and 142 Mile Creek were measured from Fort Osage, and agrees with Dr. Thurman that the site probably was 142 Mile Creek (letter 30 July).

pletely, and I returned and sat by the fire with Greenwood. He had been getting worse every day lately and this evening we began to get quite alarmed about him. His strength was entirely gone and he could hardly move. Windham & Patterson, and shortly afterwards Vansittart, brought in several turkies, one of which was immediately consigned to the tender mercies of Henry.

My little Indian mare was invaluable as a shooting poney, for with the most praiseworthy docility she would wait wherever she was left outside the cover, or in the middle of it, till one returned for her, and Windham, to whom I generally lent her on account of his rheumatism, was very fond of her.

The wood here was very fine: indeed, wherever there is much timber on these prairies the trees attain an enormous size, especially the cotton wood, post oak & hickory. The former & latter grow much like a walnut tree with fine spreading foliage: while the post oak resembles the common English oak, but is rougher and more knarled. An entomologist would have a fine field for his pursuit here: the numbers of insects, all strange to me at least, is incredible. Among the most common kinds are beetles of large size, and nearly as beautiful as the diamond beetle. If one sat down for a few minutes in a wood, one was sure to be covered with a kind of tick which insinuated themselves under the clothes, and were difficult to be got rid of. We did not see many musquitoes on account of the lateness of the season, but in summer they infest every part of the prairies. The vegetation is not so varied, at least to a superficial observer. The woods are principally composed of hickory and its varieties, cotton wood, post oak, black jack oak (which resembles a large, rough thorn without the prickles), occasionally a few filbert and hazel bushes. And, 3 or 4 species of creepers and parasitical shrubs, of which the pea vine is the largest, and which is of importance to the voyageur as being an excellent substitute for grass for horses & cattle, who are very fond of it. It is also the favourite food of deer & wild turkies.

Racoons & opossums are found wherever there is any bush, as also are otters on the streams, but we never saw any of the latter. Wild fowl of infinite variety abound in the creeks: many of them have most beautifully coloured plumage, and all are good eating. Fish are in plenty, but of few kinds. The catfish, a hideous specimen in appearance, a good deal like a miller's thumb, is the most common in the prairie streams.[67] It is found in almost all the waters of North America, and in the Western rivers is said to attain the weight of 100 lbs & upward. The largest I ever beheld was one of 17 lbs. taken at Niagara where they reach an immense size. It is scarcely fit to eat.

Poor Greenwood became dreadfully ill this evening and we could no longer doubt that he was suffering under a most alarming attack of fever & ague, probably first brought on by the wetting he got at the Parke's Camp before starting. We had not much medicine with us, but fortunately were provided with some Mercury pills, which were the best thing he could take and of which we gave him several.

[22nd]. Our invalid was so much worse this morning that we could not think of moving. He was parched with fever and the day being very hot, we could do nothing to relieve him beyond putting him on a couch round which we planted a bower of branches, and the breeze whistling among the leaves kept him tolerably cool with the assistance of some apple water. The fever seemed at the crisis and for some hours we were not without the greatest apprehension for his life. In the evening, however, we were delighted to find a little improvement in the symptoms and he was not nearly so

[67]A miller' s thumb is any of several small fresh-water, spiny-finned sculpins of Europe or North America.

feverish. We passed the time during the day in sketching, shooting and taking turns to sit with Greenwood.

I was still too weak to do much in the shooting line and spent most of the time near Greenwood, smoking and reading Shakespeare, and occasionally assisting Henry's culinary operations by peeling potatoes, onions, &c., or plucking a turkey or prairie hen. The worst part of the fever and ague is that the baneful effects of it remain for a long time after the actual sickness has left the debilitated frame, inducing the most overpowering languor and lassitude. All one's energies are utterly prostrated and the feeling is accompanied by a most ravenous, wolfish appetite. In my own case I felt at times such a complete paralysis of all my faculties that I believe if I had seen my dearest friend drowning within the reach of my hand, I could not have been at the trouble to stretch it forth to rescue him.

[23rd]. We were very glad to find Greenwood so free from fever today that at his own request we were enabled to move on a few miles. But as it was impossible he could ride, we made him up a soft couch in Vansittart's little waggon, and about 10 o'clock left 112 Mile Creek. He was annoyed by losing, just as we were starting, an enamelled breast pin, which dropped into the grass and for which we in vain searched for some time.

His couch in the waggon answered capitally, and altho completely prostrated in strength, he seemed to bear the travelling pretty well. Paterson and I rode on in front with the men and spare horses to look for a camping ground. We had a very pretty journey thro' a more hilly and better wooded country than we had for some time seen.

About 3 o'clock we passed the remains of an Indian encampment and in an hour more, on rounding the side of a hill, we suddenly came upon a lovely wooded valley, surrounded with an amphitheatre of low hills. We passed through the wood, which was about a mile across with a fine stream running through it, and crossing another creek at the Western edge, we emerged into the Prairie, and halted there as it seemed a good place for camping at. Presently Windham came up and we were gratified & surprised to learn from him that this was Council Grove, a point we had been looking forward to for some days.[68]

The waggons arriving soon afterward, we formed the camp and Windham & Paterson went out to shoot. Ridley rode in presently & told us that the mules in Vansittart's waggon would not move on and that he had left it, with Greenwood exceedingly ill, about 2 miles back. Tabaud immediately started off with a fresh mule and they soon arrived at the camp. Greenwood was put to bed & took some medicine immediately for a relapse of the fever had come on and we were more alarmed than ever and, partly on his account, partly to give the animals a rest, we resolved to remain here a day or two. There were plenty of turkeys brought in today and rumours of deer having been seen were flying about the camp, so arrangements were made for a grand chasse for tomorrow. We began, for the first time since we left the Missouri, to find the musquitoes getting troublesome, but it was the last expiring flicker of musquito existence for this year.

[24th]. Finding Greenwood a good deal better this morn-

[68]While at their previous campsite Warre had estimated the party to then be about thirty miles east of Council Grove; however, he wrote "Our distances are regulated by the mules; we give two and a half miles an hour, which is rather under the mark, but we have no other means of calculating." 54. Dr. Thurman seems correct in his view that they were camped previously at 142 Mile Creek, as they then would have been only 18 miles from Council Grove. At Warre's estimate of their rate of travel, and the time traveled that day of six hours, they would have covered fifteen miles: close enough. Had they been camped at 110 Mile Creek, they would have had a phenomenal forty miles to travel in that six hour period, with Greenwood ill in the wagon: an unlikely circumstance.

Council Grove

ing, the greater part of us went off in 3 bands to shoot. I could not keep up with my party for more than an hour or 2 and returned to camp where every thing was in a state of repose. The humm of musquitoes and an occasional distant report of a gun were the only sounds that broke the silence which pervaded our gipsy looking home. Henry & Fritz were fast asleep near the fire, which under the influence of the powerful rays of a broiling sun, was reduced to a heap of embers. The horses and cattle standing or lying among the tents, wherever they could obtain a shady spot, were dozing with drooping ears & half closed eyes, and Greenwood I was glad to find in a tranquil slumber.

I went away to the river side where I found Provost and 9 of the men making 2 caches. One was in the bank of the river, the other they made in the middle of the trail. A cache is formed by digging a large hole in the ground, which is filled with a spare stock of provisions, ammunition, &c. as a resourse in case of a party running short on their return. As soon as the holes were dug we returned to the camp where we filled 2 large bags with sugar, coffee, tea, flour, salt, &c., and a small jar of brandy was put in each. We then placed them en cache, and the earth being thrown back over them, the surface was restored as nearly as possible to its former state and we took one of the waggons two or 3 times over the one in the road to obliterate all traces of our work. The Indians are so sharpsighted that it is necessary to take the greatest care to leave no trace of a cache having been made for they have no scruple about appropriating its contents to their own use should they discover one, but it is a point of honor among the Voyageurs never to take advantage of such a trouvaille, and instances of this rule being broken through are very rare.

About dinner time the hunters came dropping in 2 or 3 at a time. They had been tolerable successful among the turkeys but had not been able to get a deer, although they had seen one which had got away and cantered across the valley close to the camp.

Greenwood continued to improve slightly.

[25th]. We did not break up the camp this morning on account of Greenwood, but in the afternoon we moved on 5 miles to a small wood which seemed a continuation of Council Grove.[69] Windham, Vansittart and Henry made a circuit, following the course of one of the creeks, & shot some turkies and prairie hen. Henry is an ardent sportsman and Vansittart is without exception the most persevering one I ever saw & shot more than any of us.

We nearly set the prairie on fire this afternoon, the dry

[69]Possibly the crossing of the Santa Fe Trail by Elm Creek, which paralleled the trail for several miles in this vicinity.

grass having caught fire by accident, and we had much trouble to extinguish it. Greenwood was much better this evening and if the weather continues as fine as lately it has been, he will soon recover.

[26th]. Being doubtful whether there was any wood at the place where we were to camp this day, we thought it advisable to carry fuel with us, and it was very fortunate we did so, for after one of the most tedious, fatiguing journeys I ever made, over a desolate waste of prairie, without seeing a single tree or a drop of water for 25 miles, with a searching Scotch Mist drizzling down upon us, we arrived at our camping ground about 7 in the evening where there was not so much as a bush. There was a fine, clear stream however, which from its peculiar brightness is called by the voyageurs, Silver Spring.[70] But from the rain, want of fire and other discomforts which we experienced there, we called the place Misery Camp.[71] Since leaving Council Grove, as we had now got into the Pawnee country, we were much more particular about the watch at night, and kept a sharp look out in the daytime.

[27th]. We were very glad to get away early this morning and continued our march over a wild hilly prairie. About 12 o'clock Fritz, who had been riding a good way ahead with Warre and Henry, came galloping back to tell us they had found a buffalo. Windham, and the rest of us, immediately rode off to the right to endeavor to see something of him, but not succeeding, we returned and kept along the trail.

Presently they came in and informed us that while riding along about a mile to the right of the trail they came up with a herd of 6 or 7 Antelopes, which they immediately gave chase

[70]It seems likely, from Fairholme's mileage estimates, that this camp was in the vicinity of present-day Lost Spring, Kansas. Marc Simmons in an undated letter [1990] agrees that Lost Spring is probably Fairholme's Silver Spring.

[71]Warre estimated the party had covered thirty miles, and his recollection was that it was a woodless camp and bad water, not at all the sparkling stream of Fairholme's description.

to. On turning the side of a hill they lost sight of the Antelope, and at the same time perceived a buffalo Bull feeding in a hollow below them. They sent back Fritz, and rode down towards the Buffalo, which made off as soon as he perceived them, and after chasing him a little distance they all of a sudden lost sight of him in so unaccountable a manner that Henry was quite persuaded that it was an Indian scout who had put on a Buffalo skin to watch us without exciting suspicion, and who on their pressing him so hard had concealed himself in the grass. From the place they found him in, this was not likely, it being quite out of sight of the trail, but as at the same time it was not impossible, it put us on the qui vive and formed an agreeable break on the monotony of the journey, for whether it was a Buffalo or an Indian, it gave us reason to expect to see more.

In the afternoon, while riding in front of the waggons, I saw Warre and Vansittart, who with Windham were about 1/2 a mile before me, suddenly dart off at full gallop to the right and when I came up to Windham, who was rolling in his saddle with laughter, I found they had gone off in pursuit of a large black wolf which had cantered past near them. In a short time they rejoined us, their horses in a foam, and told us that the quarry had crossed a little hollow into which they followed him, and instantly found their horses floundering up to their girths in a soft bog, so backing out of it as quick as possible, they contented themselves with sending a couple of shots after the wolf who, as if laughing in his sleeve at their malheur, trotted quietly up the opposite bank.

In about an hour afterwards we arrived at a fine grove on the border of a small stream named Cotton Wood Creek, from the numbers of those trees growing there, many of which were of a prodigious size: and we encamped.[72]

---

[72]Located one mile NW of present-day Durham, Kansas.

Travelling

It was here that Windham and Greenwood on their former expedition 2 years ago were overtaken while at supper by a most awful prairie fire which the Voyageurs with them said they had never seen equalled in fury and volume. Pointing to the trees above our heads Windham said "You may fancy what it was when it burnt the topmost branches of these trees." They must have been between 80 & 90 feet in height!

This was one of the pleasantest camping places we had yet seen and there were many ducks about the creek. We used the last of our fresh meat this evening, an important event in a voyageurs estimation, as a breakfast of salt bacon is a bad preparation for a days journey where you may not find water for 15 or 20 miles, and it added to our desire to reach the Buffalo country.

[28th]. We took on fuel again today and after travelling through a flat dreary country, we encamped late in the evening at a small creek where there was no wood whatever. We shot a few ducks and grouse which shed out the bacon very well, as we were not the least particular about the time our game was kept.

Henry could talk of nothing but the buffalo seen the other day, which he persisted in believing to have been and Indian, and he told us various stories of the way the Indians will dog a party for weeks together till they have a good opportunity for attacking it. Then, choosing some rough, blustering, stormy night, one or 2 of them steal in among the horses, and quietly cutting the lassos, they raise the wild and thrilling war whoop, and the others, who have been waiting within reach for the signal, dash thro the camp at full speed, screaming and yelling like fiends. When all the loosened horses taking panic, gallop off in a body into the waste where they are soon collected and taken possession of by the Indians who then have the devoted party of travellers at their mercy.

[29th]. The journey today was a more agreeable one than yesterday's, the prairie being more hilly. About 4 in the afternoon some of us were riding in the rear of the caravan when we were suddenly roused by a shout of "Buffalo" from the front, and riding up to the head of the party we found Windham, Warre, Ridley & Vansittart mounting their hunters and loading their guns. Looking in the direction pointed out, I perceived 4 large black animals about ½ a mile off, on the side of a hill. Two of them were lying down, half hidden in the long grass, the others were standing up gazing at us, but without seeming alarmed. Windham, as the most experienced, took the lead and conducted the party round under the West side of the hill, and they were soon lost to our sight in a hollow.

We remained watching the Buffalo, which were now all standing up, and presently saw the farthest one walk quickly up to the others & they all turned round, and after gazing for a moment or two behind them, huddled together like sheep, they suddenly wheeled about and gallopped off at a heavy, lumbering pace, followed at full speed by the hunters, who had now appeared over the brow of the hill.

In the middle of the chase, while the leading horseman was just closing with one of the bulls, his horse suddenly slipped and rolled over with him, & he remained on the ground, seemingly stunned. The others continued the chase and we very soon saw a shot fired by the one now in front, who was riding alongside the hindmost bull, which immediately stopped and turned savagely round on his pursuer. It was but a dying effort however, for he began to stagger, and soon sank slowly down on his knees, when another shot stretched him on the plain lifeless. The others had now disappeared over the hill, and as we had seen the dismounted horseman rise and remount his steed, we moved on and in about half an hour reached a small creek with a narrow fringe of trees along its banks where we encamped.

The hunters came in about an hour afterwards, having only shot the Buffalo we had seen killed, of which they brought the tongue and some of the meat, which Henry immediately proceeded to make into soup. It was Ridley who had been thrown, his horse having slipped in a hole, and he was a good deal stunned by the fall. The finale of the day's march put us all in high spirits this evening, besides the gratifying improvement visible in Greenwood's health, and the Canadians were charmed at the prospect of getting fresh meat for theirs had been out for some time past, as they were not so provident as Henry was of ours. Indeed it was the same with all their provisions, which lasted them only about half as long as ours did, a short life and a merry one being a true voyageur maxim.

Henry's soup was voted excellent, but the meat itself was more like leather than beef, without any fat whatever. The tongue was better, but at the time we all thought it delicious. Having drank a couple bottles of champagne which old Vogel had given Windham to wash down our first Buffalo meat, we all retired to our respective blankets to indulge in dreams of Buffalo and Pawnees. This place was called Little Arkansaw Camp, being on the creek of that name.[73]

[30th]. We remained this day here, and some of us went out to hunt and returned early, having killed 3 Buffalo Bulls.

The first Buffalo seen are always the old Bulls which, like the oldest harts among red deer, generally keep separate from (in fact I believe they are driven off by) the others in the Autumn. Those we had seen were disgusting looking animals, being very lean & mangy and as they were also changing their coats at this time, their skin looked like that of a sheep with the rot or a mangy dog, all the hair hanging loose about them in patches. In this state I think an old Bull is one of the most savage and formidable looking animals I ever beheld, but their appearance is not borne out by their character, for they are of a cowardly disposition and seldom turn upon their pursuers except when severely wounded, and not always even then.

In the spring and summer they are much more dangerous, and among themselves fight with the utmost fury at those seasons. They are about as large as a moderate sized cow, but are much deeper chested and finer in the loins, with thin flanks and clean limbs. The Bulls have immense heads, with a profusion of coarse, shaggy curling hair all over their foreheads, neck and shoulders from amidst which their little sav-

[73]Located between McPherson and Lyons, Kansas, on today's maps, and five miles south of Windom.

age looking bloodshot eyes gleam out like live coals, and with their short, thick, polished black horns standing out nearly straight from the side of their broad, shaggy foreheads to the right and left, give them a most demoniacal appearance. The general appearance of the head and forepart of the cows is much the same, only not quite as coarse looking, and being altogether lighter made, they are much faster and keep up their speed longer.

It is an error to call them Buffalo as their proper name is the Bison, or bonascus and I imagine they resemble very much the Buffalo of India and Ceylon. One would be apt to imagine from the thousands of these animals that are killed every year that their numbers must be rapidly decreasing, but the voyageurs say that they have remained about the same for the last 5 or 6 years, although for some time prior to that they were very much on the decrease. The hunting parties in the service of the Fur companies kill from 100 to 150 or 200 in a day during the hunting season, but I imagine that except when employed by the traders the Indians do not kill more than they require for food & clothing.

The winter skins of the Buffalo are used all over North America for various purposes, being thickly covered with a fine short, wooly hair, and are generally sold at from 3 to 16 or 17 dollars, according to the quality. The skin of a Bull in good condition is very handsome, being of a fine rich dark-brown colour, with a deep black tinge down the shoulders and middle of the back. Having a fine glossy appearance, they make very handsome robes for a sleigh, winter coats, rugs, &c. and form an important item in the furniture of most North Americans.

They are prepared for use by the Indians, the tanning and drying of them being the chief occupation of the squaws during the hunting season, which begins about the middle of November and lasts till the early part of the Spring. Buffalo have been domesticated but are hardly worth the trouble as the cows do not yield much milk and the flesh of the tame ones is not comparable to that of those in a wild state.

I have heard of a species of wild cattle which is said to be found in the vast forests along the Indian frontier between the Missouri and the Arkansaw rivers, but I believe them to be merely Buffalo, which are known to inhabit forest countries about the head waters of the Mississippi, and are often killed in the immense woods about the Rocky Mountains. An officer of the American Army told me at St. Louis that some years ago, when he was going up with a large detachment of troops to a station on the St. Pierre River (West of Lake Michigan) the bateaux were one day completely surrounded by a vast herd of Buffalo which were swimming across the stream, and the boats were delayed for some hours. I have no reason to class this with many other Yankee stories as I have since heard other instances of the same kind, but within the last 5 or 6 years the advance of the "Pioneers of the Far West" has driven back the Buffalo into the prairies, and they are now scarcely ever seen so far East as the St. Pierre. In the above case they were probably proceeding upon one of the periodical migrations, which there is every reason to believe they perform regularly, when they travel for weeks together in immense herds, blackening the surface of the country for miles, possibly going in search of fresh pastures.

The Pawnees and other tribes that roam over the prairies, as also the hunting Indians of the Fur companies, use principally the bow & arrow in the chase of Buffalo, and so formidable a weapon is it in their hands that they will often send the arrow quite through the animal into the ground beyond. Riding in among the herd, with as many arrows in their mouth as they can hold there, they discharge their shafts as fast as they can without waiting to kill the animals outright, and as soon as they have exhausted their stock, or find their horses blown, they return to kill and cut up the wounded which are scattered about in every direction over the prairie. In their hands the arrow is a much more murderous weapon than the gun, for the latter is at best rather inconvenient to manage on horseback at any time, but more especially when you are obliged to fire & load at full speed.

The Buffalo's fastest pace is a heavy, lumbering gallop, but it is astonishing how quickly they manage to shuffle over the ground when level, but they are soon blown in ascending a hill and, in fact, there would be no difficulty whatever in overtaking them if one's horses were kept in the same condition on the prairie as in the settlements. But after a journey of 300 or 400 miles, with little to eat besides the half-burnt prairie grasses (and sometimes scarcely even that if you have to go over a burnt prairie) horses do not come up to Buffalo in racing condition, and the Indian horses, altho' very hardy & possessed of great bottom, are much too small to carry a man very fast for any distance. From our carrying corn with us, our horses were probably in better condition than the same number ever were before so far out on the prairie, and altho' the ox waggon was the cause of some delay & trouble to us from the slow pace at which it proceeded, yet we were amply repaid in the fine appearance of our steeds.

While at full speed the Buffalo carries his tail erect in the air, but when he is wounded or hard pressed, it is often observed to extend out horizontally with a little upward curve in the middle & in that state the voyageurs call it the Mad Tail, and the animal is then a dangerous customer should he close with you.

[October 1st]. We broke up the camp early today and proceeded over a fine, open rolling prairie, seeing a good many small detached bands of Buffalo, till about 3 o'clock when we encamped on a flat piece of ground near a small creek, along the banks of which grew a few trees and some underwood. As I was unable to hunt, I lent old Cendre to Paterson who with some of the others, forthwith went off to a small herd which we had observed near the camp. Greenwood & I amused ourselves as we best could till 6 o'clock, when all the party having returned except Paterson, we sat down to dinner. They had killed 4 or 5 Bulls, of which they brought home the tongues, but since the beginning of the hunt none of them had seen Paterson As we knew he had no compass with him we became rather uneasy when 8 o clock came & no Paterson, but at length, about 9, just as we were thinking of sending off in search of him, we were delighted to see the worthy General ride into the Camp. My poor old Cendre looked quite done up, and no wonder for Paterson had killed 5 bulls, which considering that he rode at least 15 stone,[74] was a very tolerable afternoon's work for one horse, as each bull takes about 20 minutes hard gallopping.

Paterson told us that he had got so excited with the sport that he forgot to look out for the trail, and consequently when he turned his face homewards, instead of being 2 or 3 miles to the South of it as he supposed, he was some distance to the North. After wandering about the Prairie for some time he was fain to throw the reins on old Cendre's neck and let him find his own way, which he did beautifully to the no small gratification of his rider, for it was coming on to be very cold and by no means the kind of night one would have chosen to sleep out on the open Prairie.

Windham & Greenwood made themselves a snuggery on the bank of the creek among the underwood where they lit a fire and hung a mat (one of our tablecloths) over the branches in case of rain, and the rest retired to the tents.

[74]In British measure, a "stone" equals fourteen pounds, so Paterson at "15 stone" weighed 210 pounds.

[2nd]. In the middle of the night Paterson & I were most rudely awoke by our tent's being blown down upon us and when we had extricated ourselves from the mass of canvass, which was soaking wet, we discovered that we were completely exposed to a most pitiless storm of snow, sleet & rain, with a violent wind blowing.

He ran off to Windham's bower & I was hospitably received into the other tent where we were very cosy till about 5 in the morning, when it also was blown down and we all scampered off to the general refuge for the destitute [known] as the Hotel Windham, where we sat shivering & smoking till Henry had prepared us some strong coffee, after which, having christened this place Snow Camp, we woke up the encampment & advanced 5 miles to a small creek where we halted for a more substantial Breakfast. There were thousands of ducks and teal here, and Ridley & Vansittart having remained behind for an hour to shoot after we had left it, killed without difficulty 12 couple. We were all beginning to be much afflicted with dysentery proceeding, as we imagined, from the quantity of mud in the water we had been using for the last 2 days, which while boiling, threw up a thick white scum on the surface.

This day was very fine but with a slight frosty feeling, and we began to see great numbers of wild swans, geese & cranes high up in the air, winging their way from the cold regions of Hudsons Bay & the Red river country towards the milder Southern climates to which they emigrate for the Winter.

Their wild, melancholy cries, particularly those of the geese which, proceeding from thousands of these birds & mellowed by the great distance they were above our heads [creating] a most mournfully musical effect, reminded us of the approach of winter & gave a more desolate cast to the scenery of the bleak prairie, dotted with small bands of Buffalo, over which we were travelling.

We halted about 6 in the evening, on the banks of a fine stream, with plenty of wood about it, named Cow Creek.[75] Having come about 25 miles we had not attempted to kill any Buffalo on the way as it was quite a long enough day's work for the horses without hunting & we wished to reserve their energies for the grand hunts when we should arrive among the main herds, which we now expected very soon to do.

We got a few shots at the wild geese this evening as they flew over the camp, but without any effect from the great height they were above us. Henry made a capital stew of some of the ducks shot in the morning which were in fine order and very fat. I should have liked much to have preserved the skins of some of them as besides being very beautiful, I imagine many of these prairie ducks are little known. Indeed, I had got a bottle of arsenical soap for the purpose from the museum at Niagara, but my illness made me so listless that I never could bear the trouble. We had seen but few prairie hen lately, and no wild turkeys since we left Council Grove. I believe the latter are not found on the prairies west of that place until you come to the Rocky Mount^{n}s.

It is curious that the Americans should have selected the Bald Eagle as the national Emblem when they might have chosen such a noble bird as the wild turkey, which also is indigenous to America. Franklin was very averse to the selection of the former, its character being treacherous, rapacious & cowardly, while the wild turkey is a bird of great courage in combat, and dignified & harmless in peace, a fit emblem for a nation. Perhaps, however, the habits of the eagle are more in unison with the character of the people he represents.

[3rd]. We kept today along the downward course of Cow Creek, seeing plenty of Bulls, of which we killed 2. For the last 2 or 3 days, we had observed all the valleys & watercours-

[75]Located four miles west of present-day Lyons, Kansas.

es incline, instead of to the North & North-West, to the South of us, a sign that we had reached the summit of the land between the Missouri and Arkansas.[76] We saw more wood today than yesterday, and except the vast flights of wild-fowl, all symptoms of winter had disappeared and a scorching sun beat down on us as if it was July instead of October, which was all the better for us as nothing knocks up horses so much as exposure to the cold, frosty winds of the Fall on the prairies.

We had a fine chase in the middle of the day, after an outlying deer, which was startled from his lair in a little hollow in the prairie, and gave us a smart burst for a few minutes. Windham got a shot at him, after which we did not see him again, so it may be presumed he got away scot free. After a journey of about 18 miles we encamped again on Cow Creek, which was here much larger, with a great deal of wood along its banks.[77]

[4th]. We started very early this morning in hopes of reaching the Arkansaw, along the banks of which we expected to find plenty of Buffalo and, accordingly, after travelling about 12 miles we came to the edge of a high table land, from whence we were rewarded by a splendid prospect.

Below us extended for many miles, stretching away to the West, a rich flat valley, down the middle of which glided the broad, smooth Arkansaw, bordered with noble woods in some places scattered, & in others hiding the stream altogether from our view. The left side of the valley was formed of a remarkable chain of high table lands, presenting towards

[76]Simmons noted that the Cow Creek area marked the boundary between the tallgrass country to the east, and the shortgrass country running westward from that point. The shortgrass range was the home of the buffalo (95).

[77]The Kansas State Historical Society *Eighteenth Biennial Report* (115) identifies two Cow Creek camps: the first called "Branch of Cow Creek," and the one on which the party was now camped was apparently the "Main Cow Creek." The table of distances indicates it is fifteen miles to the Arkansas River from that camp, and an additional fifty-two miles to the Pawnee Fork.

the river an almost precipitous appearance, and as they receded from it, towards our right, were broken into numberless little ravines and valleys on whose rounded sides we could distinguish large herds of Buffalo, looking in the distance almost like dark stains on the prairie.

Beyond these high lands was an immense flat plain on which seemed to be a small lake, (but this we afterwards found to have been an effect of mirage caused by the intense heat of the sun) and which extended far away to the N. & N.W., till on the very horizon it merged into a faint line of low hills, which were barely distinguishable in the distance. The right side of the valley was low and covered for some distance with wood, beyond which the prairie undulated away to the South, looking like the ocean subsiding after a gale, which resemblance was strengthened by the marvellous effect of the mirage, a common phenomenon on the prairies, as in the deserts of the East.

About 8 or 9 miles up the valley a narrow blue fringe of wood indicated the course of the Pawnee Fork, a small tributary of the Arkansaw. Immediately below us was a large marsh, in which great numbers of cranes & wild geese were alighting, and the whole valley was sprinkled with Buffalo in small bands, or scattered about singly, on the banks of the Arkansaw.

Altogether it was such a view as once seen can never be forgotten & to which no pencil could ever hope to do justice. Descending from the heights into the valley, we passed thro the marsh where Windham stalked & shot a fine ontarde, or Canada Goose, and in about 2 hours we were encamped on a small flat piece of land on the edge of the river with Buffalo bulls all round us, seemingly not very much disturbed by our proximity. All the prairie near the river was intersected by hundreds of little paths, like sheep-paths, which are made by

Valley of the Arkansas

the Buffalo, who generally, in high grass, walk in single file, which they keep very regularly. Various plans were in agitation for the morrow's sport, and even Greenwood & I, although not in very good working condition, resolved to try our strength & our horses among the cows.

[5th]. As soon as Breakfast was over we were all engaged cleaning our guns & pistols, sharpening knives, and other preparations for the hunt. Old Provost & Windham scanned the sides of the hills with a telescope & discovered about 3 miles N.W. of us a large herd, amidst which they thought they could distinguish some cows & calves, and it was resolved that our first attempt should be made in that direction. Accordingly, about 10 o'clock we all set out, mounted

on our best horses, & accompanied by Tabaud & 2 others of the men, on ponies, leading mules bearing pack saddles, on which was to be carried home the meat from any Buffalo we might kill. We proceeded at an easy pace across the flat haugh between the river & the rising grounds, which we commenced ascending about a mile east of the herd.

It was necessary to keep a sharp lookout among the grass for rattlesnakes, of which there were great numbers. At one time I almost rode over a monster of near 6 feet long, which was lying right in my path, but I just saw him in time. It is fortunate that they are generally found in the barest places and on dry, sandy spots where they lie basking in the sun, so that with a little care one can easily avoid them, & they rarely attack without receiving provocation.

The Buffalo were on the side of a pretty steep hill, near the top, and just under them was a deep narrow ravine, up whose west side if we could steal unperceived, we should come upon the top of the hill within 100 yards of the herd. The wind luckily favoured our doing this, and having descended from where we had made our observations, we were soon stealing up, as quietly as possible, along the bottom of the ravine, Windham leading the way.

It was a moment of intense excitement when, leaving the bottom, we struck straight up the steep bank, and peering over the top, found ourselves within 70 or 80 yards of the herd. With much pleasure we perceived a great many cows & calves among the bulls. They were all lying down, or standing dozing in the sun & chewing the cud, and on the outskirts some steady old Bulls seemed stationed as centinels. Three of those were close to where we came up and hearing the noise we made, they turned and gazed at us in startled astonishment for a moment, and gallopped off towards the rest, who on their approach instantly roused themselves, collected

Shooting Buffaloe

together in a dense body, and in a minute or two the whole herd were thundering away from us at full speed, cows, Bulls & calves mingled together and making the ground shake as with the charge of a Regiment of Cavalry & jostling each other in a compact dark mass, with their tails erected high in the air, to the number, I should think, of about 500.

We had no time to make any philosophical observations then, for the moment we perceived that there were cows among them Windham gave the word "Now away you go!" and by the time the Buffalo were in motion we were in full chase. The ground for the 1st ¼ of a mile was pretty good along the top of the hill, and we tore along, "a pleine bride," as if it was the first burst of a pack of fox hounds, but the excitement was ten times greater, and I felt almost mad at first, but when the Buffalo took down the hill, which was rather steep & very rough, I became hardly able to sit in my saddle from weakness, and was most reluctantly obliged to pull up and go quietly down.

By this time, the herd had divided into three, each with 2 horsemen after it, and as they swept up the opposite side of the valley below me the horses gained fast upon them, & I saw 2 or 3 shots fired. The chase then turned over the top of the hill & soon disappeared from my view, but 2 buffalo lay dead on the prairie, and a third, mortally wounded, was staggering along the side of the brae.

I immediately rode slowly down into the valley where I met Tabaud & the other men, who after I had dispatched the wounded cow, proceeded to take the meat from all three, and pack it on the mules. I left them thus engaged and followed in the direction taken by the hunt, but when I reached the top of the rise not a vestige of them was to be seen, except another cow lying dead a few yards from me. I rode on at an easy canter, till coming to a higher place than the rest of the ground I perceived, about a mile off, a small detached body of the Buffalo, with one horseman riding close at their heels. They seemed quite blown, and were going very slowly, while the hunter appeared to be riding among them to pick out the fattest. I afterward found this was Windham who shot 2 of the best cows.

Hearing someone call at a little distance below me, I looked down into the valley & saw Ridley standing near a wounded cow at Bay. I immediately joined him, & found he had lost his caps and could not kill her, but with my gun he soon gave her coup de grace.[78] We could not cut her up artis-

[78]This reference would indicate the party was using percussion cap guns, not flintlocks. Many of the mountain men of this era continued to use the flintlock for this very reason.

tically, so contenting ourselves with taking the tongue, we remounted our steeds, & turned their heads homeward.

It was by this time nearly 4 o'clock, and as we were still in the valley of the Arkansaw about 5 miles above the camp, we proceeded leisurely and arrived about ½ past 5, being the first home except Greenwood, who something like me had found himself too weak to continue the chase long but had, however, killed a very fine cow in the early part of the run. He had also had a great misfortune for thinking he could shoot better with a pistol at such close quarters He left his gun with Tabaud, who happened to be near him after he had shot the Buffalo, and continued the chase, but in the act of firing one of his pistols, his hand dropped from mere weakness & the ball went thro' the neck of his horse. He was riding the little mare he got from me and the wound, altho not so bad as he at first feared, was quite sufficient to prevent his using her again for hunting. It was the more annoying as he was quite delighted with her, for she seemed to understand the work perfectly, and was an exceedingly pleasant goer.

My horse, Cendre, altho' the only properly trained Buffalo horse of the party, was a most unfortunate steed for a sick man to ride. His action, even at a walk, was so dreadfully rough that it used to shake me to pieces, and in going down hill particularly, I sometimes felt quite sick with a most painful oppressed feeling in my forehead, as if it was splitting, an effect which I attribute to the quantity of mercury I had taken.

By dinner time the whole party had reassembled & we had various accounts of the days sport. The number of Buffalo killed was 9, of which 5 had been "arrangees" by the Canadians, and at dinner we all agreed that the meat of the cows was the most delicious we had ever eaten, very fat & tender. The men had taken care to bring all the marrow bones, a favourite prairie delicacy, and the fires were filled with them. The orthodox way of cooking them being to thrust them, with a good deal of meat on them, into the embers, and when cooked enough, you first eat the meat off and then use the marrow as butter for your biscuits or bread. This is the true way of eating marrowbones, whether of Buffalo on the prairies or of moose in the Canadian forests.[79]

We were all very well satisfied with the days sport, for even I had enjoyed myself excessively altho' I was the only unsuccessful one of the party, and all the others were in high spirits with this good beginning.

[6th]. The day was cold and lowering, and we did not move till late, when we proceeded up the Arkansaw about a mile and encamped among a few trees in a kind of bottom close by the River. All round us the grass was exceedingly high, so much so in some places to conceal a man on horseback. The whole of this low valley seems to be flooded by the rise of the river in Spring, being full of holes in which the water was still remaining. There were plenty of Bulls near the camp, but we did not molest them.

I was annoyed at finding both Cendre & my little Indian mare very much saddle-galled this evening. By Tabaud's advice I filled up the wounds with wood ashes, which by the Canadians are held to be a sovereign remedy for cuts and bruises.

In the middle of the night we were much alarmed by a

[79]Warre originally commented extensively on the expedition's "menu," in his book; however in the proof copy his comments were nullified by being entirely scratched out. The deleted paragraph reads: "With our good living, which we enjoy with the far-famed 'hunter's appetite,' it is not surprising that some of us sometimes complain of indigestion....The following bill of fare will give a specimen of our food—Soup thickened with onions and beans, followed by a rôti of beef; the boudins being the tenderloin mashed with potatoes, onions, &c; a cow's udder (the sight of which was enough to bring on a fit of the gout) and marrow bones. Our snacks consisted of stewed apples and pancakes....Tea and coffee with hot scones baked in a hole under the fire completed a repast I have seldom seen excelled, and certainly never enjoyed with greater gusto."

large herd of Buffalo, which collected on the opposite side of the river and commenced swimming across, right down upon the camp. It was a very picturesque scene, the river being full of buffalo (whose splashing & hard breathing we could hear distinctly), while the dark woods throwing the opposite side into deep shadow gave a mysterious uncertainty to their proceedings. On our shore the sparkling water was illuminated by the fitful glare of several large fires which we had lighted along the bank to scare the Buffalo, and from the shouting & occasional reports of guns which we fired now & then, one might have supposed the camp to be attacked by Indians.

About the middle of the stream was a large sandbank, on which the herd landed & stood for a short time looking at us, when not being exactly able to make us out, & probably considering omne ignutum jus terribils, they divided into 2 or 3 bodies, some going back and the others landing below us. One bull tried to go up, but being carried down by the current, landed close to the camp & immediately gallopped off, passing very near to the horses, & causing us some alarm lest they should be seized with a panic: fortunately, however, they took no notice of him.

If this herd had continued their traverse and landed in the camp, we should to a certainty have lost, for a time at all events, many of our horses & mules & perhaps some of us might have been killed, for where Buffalo once make a rush in a herd, nothing will stop them, & it was probably only their being forced to stop & land in the middle of the river that saved us.

[7th]. We remained here this day. I found that the wood ashes had answered their purpose admirably, both Cendre & the poney being nearly recovered.

All the party except Greenwood & I went out hunting. As he had not recovered the fatigue of our last hunt, he remained in camp all day, but I mounted my Indian mare & rode quietly up the bank of the Arkansaw to some marshy ground where I thought I might find some snipes & ducks, but I was disappointed. I was riding nearly the whole time through grass which I could barely see over, and while returning I suddenly emerged from the high grass & was rather startled at seeing close in front of me 5 large old Buffalo Bulls. They were at least as much astounded at my appearance as I was at seeing them, and immediately made off. I followed for about 20 minutes, but becoming unable to keep up at the necessary speed, I fired two long shots at them, watched them till they disappeared in the vain hope that my shots might have told, and then wended my way homeward.

When I got to camp I was completely done up, so having turned the poney out, I joined Greenwood, who was sitting by the fire reading the Arabian Nights' Entertainments (lent to him by Henry) and occasionally varying the monotony of his occupation by cooking little kabobs of Buffalo meat. I being very hungry, improved on his cookery by getting the frying pan, & made a very substantial luncheon, which lasted at intervals till near dinnertime. This voracity was one of the disagreeable effects of the fever, but we were not aware of that at the time, & consequently astonishing our companions by the quantity we devoured.

The others all came in by 6 o'clock, having killed 2 Bulls and one cow. We were dreadfully tormented by dysentery during the whole time we were on the Arkansaw. Some attributed it to the inordinate quantity of rich, succulent fresh meat which we ate, but more probably it was the muddy quality of the water of the river which threw up a thick scum while being boiled, a common occurrence with the water of almost all prairie streams.

As to the first conjecture, no one could believe the quantity of meat eaten at an encampment of hunters in the Buffalo country. Go into the camp at what time you choose [and] you were sure to find 2 or 3 of the party roasting or frying titbits of the meat, and the flesh of the cows & young Bulls is rich & juicy beyond any I ever saw. The best venison is not to be compared to it and as we had plenty of other things to eat, our partiality for it cannot be attributed to any want of variety in our food. The Canadians were perfectly happy: fine weather, plenty of tobacco, and as much buffalo meat as he can eat, constituting the seventh heaven of a voyageur.

[8th]. As the main herds had been driven off a little by the last 2 days hunting, we thought it advisable to move up a few miles higher, especially as we expected to get better pasture for the mules & horses. So, after breakfast, we proceeded 6 miles up the valley and encamped in a little peninsula formed by the windings of the Pawnee fork, which surrounded us on 3 sides, while on the fourth was a tolerably thick grove of trees.[80] We shot a few ducks on the way, but by the time we arrived it was too late to go out hunting; however, from the camp we could see a great many Buffalo about 4 miles up to the Northwest. We were not without apprehension of the Pawnees here, & chose our position as making it difficult to carry off our horses by a coup-de-main, as there was plenty of pasture and room for them close to the camp, & within the peninsula.

As for a fight, we were more than a match for 3 or 4 times our number, being so much better armed than any of the Indian tribes in this part of the Prairies. The Comanches, whose country borders upon that of the Pawnees not very far South from the Pawnee fork, are a very brave & warlike nation, inhabiting principally the prairies South of the Arkansaw. But, as they are not so well armed as the Pawnees,

---

[80]This site is at present-day Larned, Kansas. It seems strange that Fairholme made no mention of Pawnee Rock as they traveled this stretch of the river. Pawnee Rock was perhaps the most outstanding natural feature in the area at that time, and a landmark for travelers on the Santa Fe Trail.

we were less afraid of falling in with them, besides, the Pawnees being a much more treacherous, thieving set than the others, require to be more carefully guarded against, and we were here in the very heart of their country.

[9th]. A wretched day. The rain never ceased and we all remained in inglorious idleness in Camp, except Vansittart, whose unvarying ardour induced him to go out after the Buffalo. He returned about 3 o'clock, wet through, but had been amply rewarded by killing 2 cows. Not satisfied with this, as soon as he had sent off one or 2 of the men to fetch home the meat, he took his gun again and walked away to look for wild ducks about the river near camp. He had not been gone 5 minutes when we heard him fire a shot, and immediately begin shouting to us. Some of us ran up, expecting to find a whole tribe of Pawnees at the least, but were very glad to see him standing over a fine deer which he had put up within 100 yards of our fires. It was a doe, & we immediately bore her into the camp rejoicing, being the first deer we had killed. She was precisely similar to the common deer of Canada, but at dinner no one thought of the venison while there was Buffalo meat.

Vansittart also shot 2 racoons during the afternoon, and we tried their flesh, but altho it looked like the finest pork, it had a strong rank taste, & was not approved of at our table, altho the Canadians liked it.

[10th]. Windham, Vansittart & I went out to hunt Buffalo today, and found a fine herd about 5 miles from the camp. They were on the side of a hill, & we had some difficulty in getting up to them. Just as we got within about 300 yards of them they suddenly started off without any visible cause (for they could not see us, nor could they scent us, as we kept well to leeward of them), and we were obliged to follow with a very bad start, but in about 20 minutes we were alongside of and amongst them.

I was just beginning to feel it was time to pull up, and at about 15 yards from the outside of the herd I fired off both barrels at random. It was all I could do to raise the gun to my shoulder, and the moment I fired I stopped for I could not have gone 20 yds further without falling off from utter weakness, & I had not even the consolation of seeing that either shot had taken effect. It was deeply provoking and I eased my conscience by giving sundry maledictions to the night I slept in the rain at the Osage river. However, there was no help for it. I reloaded and followed slowly in the direction they had taken, but after riding mile or two without seeing anything of them, I began to think of returning.

Striking across the prairie to the South I arrived, after an hours riding, in the Valley of the Pawnee fork, and perceiving two or 3 horsemen a long way off above me I remained quiet till, finding they were friends, I joined them. It proved to be Tabaud & Pierre, who were returning from 2 cows which Vansittart had killed about a mile higher up the valley, the herd having turned to the South after I stopped, and crossed the Pawnee Fork, and Arkansaw.

We rode on together for some distance when I perceived, on a bare sandy spot, some little animals like rabbits running to & fro, as if in a great bustle, and others sitting up on their hind legs. I got off my horse, and followed by Pierre, stole quietly up to get a shot at them, but just as I was taking aim at 3 of them, altogether a beautiful shot, I was startled by a loud cry from Pierre. The prairie dogs, as they are called, disappeared instantly, their heels twinkling for a moment in the air as they dived into their holes, and I looked round to Pierre, who screamed out, "Le serpent! Gardez-vous du serpent!" And there, sure enough, close at my feet was a large rattlesnake advancing toward me with his head up in the air, and his eyes sparkling like diamonds. I made off immediately, and when a few paces off, waited to see what he would do. He came on in the most graceful undulations till he arrived at the mouth of one of the prairie dog burrows, which he seemed inclined to enter. But as he had spoiled my sport, I took advantage of his pause to take a shot at him. My ball cut his head clean off, and his body remained twisting & writhing for a long time afterwards.

I sat down with Pierre to wait till the little creatures should show themselves again, and presently one popped his head out of a hole, then another, and they seemed to hold a consultation together for a short time, when they both came out and sat up on their hind legs in the most comical way, opposite each other, till two or 3 others joined them. It was really very amusing to watch the bustling manner they all ran about from hole to hole, as if paying visits of congratulation on the danger being past, for they could not see us, we being concealed behind a thick bush of grass. I put an end to their gossipping after I had watched them for a little time by firing a ball into the middle of them (having no shot with me). I was almost sorry to see that I had severely wounded one which, just like a rabbit, managed to scramble into a hole close to him, and after a fruitless attempt to get him, we remounted our horses and pursued our route.

These prairie dogs seem to be a species of marmot. Their villages are always in bare spots, & generally on a slight eminence from which they can see around them, and it would seem that the rattlesnakes live with them, for they are invariably found together. I have several times seen a snake enter a hole into which one of the prairie dogs had gone a short time before. There is also a very diminutive species of owl* which is supposed to live with them also, but we did not see any. If it is the case, it is a very remarkable fact that a bird, a serpent & a quadruped sh/d inhabit the same den, more particularly as I

*Fairholme's note: Strix Cunnicularia (Wilson & Bonaparte). They are also common in parts of the West Indies, and are known as the Burrowing Owl.

should imagine there can be no doubt that the rattlesnake feeds on the prairie dog.

Shortly after we left the prairie dog village we were overtaken by Windham, who came down the valley. He told us that after I gave up the chase the herd divided, Vansittart following one part, & he the other. Just as he was coming up with the Buffalo (for being badly mounted this day, he had not kept so close to them as Vansittart and I at first) he perceived at some distance from him what seemed to be 2 or 3 horsemen, and being in doubt who they were, he thought it prudent not to discharge his gun in case they were Indians. He therefore let the Buffalo get away, but on examining the horses more particularly, he thought it was Tabaud & Pierre, one of the animals being grey, and Pierre being mounted on a grey mule. However, they were so far off that he could not be certain, so he rode cautiously up, till he came within ½ a mile of them when he perceived that they were without riders. Thinking they were some of our horses got away by accident from the camp, he approached till he distinguished that they certainly did not belong to us, and that they were in fact, wild horses. He went up close to them without their showing any alarm, merely snorting and trotting round him for a few minutes, when probably "smelling the smell of an Englishman," they took fright and gallopped off. Their action he described as beautiful and one of them, a brown horse, was really a very fine animal. The other was a stout grey poney, and had an Indian brand on his flank, showing that at some time he had been in possession of the Pawnees. Tabaud was highly delighted at hearing this and they settled to go out very early tomorrow with lassos and endeavour to catch one, which Windham promised to Tabaud, if they succeeded.

Just as we came in sight of the camp I perceived about 500 yards from us 3 white looking animals under a little mound which I took for white wolves, and pointed them out to

Windham & Tabaud, who the moment he saw them exclaimed that they were Antelopes. The grass was pretty high & favoured our stalking them, so Windham & I dismounted and told the men to remain perfectly still with the horses. We then set off thro' the long grass, on our hands & knees & had gotten within 120 yards of them, when we perceived them start, look round & bound off like the wind. We gave them our 4 barrels, but without effect, and returned to our horses, one of which having moved, had been seen by the antelope who instantly took the alarm. They were very pretty creatures, of a pale grey colour, and seemed shaped like the African Antelope, only rather larger.

As soon as we reached camp we discovered the reason of the Buffalo having started off in so unusual a manner when we first came up with them in the morning. Warre & Ridley had gone out to hunt about ½ an hour after we did, & forgetting to take advantage of the wind, they had advanced straight upon the Buffalo instead of going round to leeward as we did. The consequence was natural: the Buffalo whose sense of smell is exceedingly acute, scented them when they must have been at least ½ a mile off & took flight, as we had cause to observe.

Warre & Ridley had gone away North & had shot nothing, seeing only one or two old Bulls. On their return Warre went down to the Arkansaw to water his horse and got a shot at an Antelope, which he missed. It was a buck, and he described its horns as being straight & wrinkled like those of the African Antelope. I could not distinguish any on those we saw, but they were going too fast to enable me to distinguish them very particularly. We found numbers of skeletons & bones of buffalo scattered all over these prairies, particularly the broad osfrontis with the horns still remaining on, that bone being too hard for even the wolves to make a dinner of. In fact, at a very little distance it will turn a leaden bullet. These remains seemed to prove that we were in a favourite hunting ground & the great numbers of buffalo there favours this supposition.

[11th]. Windham & Tabaud went off early this morning to endeavour to catch one or 2 of the wild horses. After breakfast, we moved up the Pawnee Fork about 5 miles & encamped in a nice flat meadow surrounded on 3 sides by the river with a fringe of prodigious cotton wood trees.[81] We lighted our fire under a group of 4 or 5 of them which must have been between 80 & 90 feet high, with immensely thick stems and branches. The front of the camp was open towards the prairie, & there was good pasture within its limits.

I rode out by myself on to the hills, in search of a prairie dog village, which I did not succeed in finding, but when about 4 miles above the camp, on mounting a pretty steep rise from which I had a very extended view, I beheld an enormous herd of Buffalo in the act of crossing the valley. They were going at full speed, and crossed the Pawnee Fork & Arkansaw, and in the plain beyond the latter they joined another vast herd, and in a few minutes the whole were in rapid motion. To call it herd would give no idea of the thousands of Buffalo: the whole plain was literally black with them, and quite in the van, and a little apart from them, was a considerable troop of wild horses, but from the distance they were at I could merely distinguish that they were horses. I should think that at the smallest computation there must have been between 5 and 6000 animals, all moving in a vast black mass across the prairie to the S.W. and I watched them till I could distinguish nothing but a dark blotch on the plain, which was soon lost to sight altogether.

[81] Still in the immediate vicinity of Larned, Kansas.

I could not conceive what had alarmed them for I had seen no pursuers, and as it might have been a hunting party of pawnees, I thought it prudent to proceed homeward. I found that Warre, Ridley & Vansittart had likewise seen them from another part of the hills, about a mile nearer camp than I was, but as they had observed nothing to account for their precipitate flight we presumed that they had been seized with a panic, an occurrence which often takes place both with the Buffalo & wild horses.

They had found on the hills several hares, which they chased, & one of which Vansittart killed by a beautiful shot with a ball. It resembled in all respects the common English hare, and as there are none either in Canada or the United States (except a few which have been imported) we were exceedingly surprised at finding them out on these wild prairies. Henry & Paterson's man had also been out shooting during the day, and shot 3 or 4 prairie dogs, but they saw no Buffalo except 3 or 4 old Bulls, which nobody ever thought of wasting powder & shot on while there were cows to be had.

Windham & Tabaud came in just before dinner. They had found the horses about 6 miles up the valley and as soon as they perceived them they tied Greenwood's mare (which they had taken for the purpose) within sight of the horses & retired into a little hollow near her. As soon as they left the mare by herself she began to neigh, hearing which the wild ones came trotting up till within 70 or 80 yards of her, when they both stopped, neighed in reply, trotted about her backwards & forwards, but seeming to suspect treachery would not come nearer. Windham seeing this, told Tabaud to take the mare & follow him, and then dashed up toward the wild horses, who made off at full gallop. He pursued them, lasso in hand, for about a mile & a half as hard as his horse could lay legs to the ground & soon came up within 80 yards of the grey, which was not so fast as the other. Windham was fully prepared to throw the lasso over him in another 100 yards, but there is many a slip twixt the cup & the lip: his horse, which had been going slightly lame the whole day, at this critical juncture made a false step, & when he recovered himself he was dead lame, and Windham was obliged to relinquish his prize just as he seemed on the point of securing it.

It was a great pity, for if Windham's horse could have held out 10 minutes longer the wild one was so blown that he must have given in to the superior blood & bone of his pursuer, which was a very fine, wellbred animal, like an Irish hunter in appearance. They came home very slowly, and the chesnut was not fit for work for several days after. The weather continued beautiful: fine sunny days, not too hot, much like September weather in England.

[12th]. Being a good deal knocked up, & feeling languid today, I remained in camp with Greenwood, who had latterly been quite incapable of any exertion. So we smoked & read & cooked Buffalo meat all day till the rest of the party came in. They had a pretty good day's sport, having killed 4 cows & some bulls. We did not keep much count of the Bulls, as when killed at all it was generally by mistake, as there is not so very marked a difference between them & the cows, but young hands like us were liable to fire at the one for the other, especially if the Bull was a young one.

[13th]. Greenwood & I kept each other company again today, while the others went out. We found it necessary to move the camp about ½ a mile down the Creek to get at better pasture. This afforded us some occupation & when the men had taken away all the tents, waggons, &c., he & I remained at the fire watching the hundreds of ravens & turkey-buzzards, which assembled to feast upon the bones & refuse which were scattered all about the place. They did not care the least for our presence, but hopped about within a few

yards of us, fighting bitterly for the larger pieces of meat, &c. As a great exertion, we agreed to walk down the creek to the new camp. It took us nearly ½ an hour to accomplish this feat (the distance being about ½ a mile), and when we got in we were both quite exhausted.

I took my gun out in the afternoon and crawled, rather than walked, about the river in hopes of killing some ducks, but I did not get a shot so near the camp. The others came in at dinner time after a splendid day's hunting, having killed 8 cows and some Bulls. But they had to go a long way to get them as the main herd seemed to begin to find our propinquity disagreeable and kept a more respectful distance than when we first came.

A lengthened discussion took place this evening as to the propriety of having sugar with our brandy and water at night. Greenwood maintained that we ought only to have sugar with our tea & coffee at breakfast & dinner & would not even hear of allowing those who chose to go without sugar [at meals] in order to have sweet brandy & water, or hot stocking as we called it, at night.[82] After a keen encounter of wits, it was agreed that the next day's allowance of sugar should be served out to each at night so that every man might make such use of his allowance as he thought proper.

The importance of the discussion is only to be appreciated at 400 to 500 miles from a grocer's shop. Henry was quite invaluable: every now & then he would produce butter, eggs, or some other luxury which we did not know of his having, & which was the more agreeable. We tried the milk of the Buffalo, but there was very little to be got from them & not good.

[14th]. We treated ourselves this morning to two Buffalo humps and found them exceedingly good. The meat itself is

[82]Earlier in his journal Fairholme referred to it as "hot stopping."

very small, but is enclosed in a large mass of fat, which in fact forms the hump. As we had agreed to keep all the humps & tongues for our friends in Canada, we did not infringe upon our stock very often.

We moved camp today to the Arkansaw, to the place where we camped on the 6th. But as it was about the last day we sh[d] have a chance of killing any cows, we all went out, except poor Greenwood, who seemed to get more languid every day. We proceeded up to the hills, which we ascended about 2 miles N.W. of the camp, but were bitterly disappointed. Not a single Buffalo was to be seen in any direction, except 4 old Bulls, which kept cantering on about ½ a mile ahead of us the whole day. We rode along the plain at the back of the hills without seeing any herds. The only animals we saw were some large gaunt looking white wolves and a number of cranes & pelicans which were stationed all along a piece of water in the middle of the plain, apparently fishing, & which I at first took for Antelopes.

About 4 o'clock we struck across the prairie towards the Arkansaw and on the top of one of the hills had some good fun gallopping after 3 or 4 hares, none of which however did we succeed in killing as we had nothing but ball with us. Descending into the valley of the Arkansaw, we came upon our friends the 4 Bulls. For want of better sport we gave chase to them & Warre & I selected by chance the same Bull, which after 10 minutes gallop he wounded. The Buffalo immediately stopped, and then made a most savage charge at him, when I gave Bully his coup-de-grace. Ridley & Vansittart had each killed one before long, & we cut out the tongues & left the bodies for the wolves.

While riding towards the new camping ground Windham shot a rattlesnake in which there seemed a remarkable swelling, and on opening him we found an immense rat, apparently just swallowed for the fur was scarcely ruffled, but it was as limber as a kid glove, every bone in its body being crushed.

Windham's horse got away while we were examining the rat, & we had some trouble in catching him, but were rewarded for it by putting up, during our chase of him, some prairie hen of which we shot 3, and then rode into the camp. Just as we entered it I looked back at the carcases of the Buffalo, and saw 6 or 7 black wolves, besides some little prairie wolves, already tearing at them while three large white ones were stealing along under the rising ground towards the feast. Not a wolf was to be seen but ½ an hour before & where they all came from in so short a time is a mystery to me. The prairie wolf resembles slightly a jackall, & lives in burrows on the prairie, but I do not think the other wolves do so, at this season at least.

We were much annoyed to find that on the way from the Pawnee Fork a wheel of one of the waggons had broken, and when we entered the camping ground they were only just beginning to light the fires, having been delayed some time by this untoward mischance. The evening was dark & threatening, & looked as if it prognosticated a change in the weather.

[15th]. This morning set in with a violent storm of wind, thunder & rain which continued without intermission all day. Poor Tabaud had been up late last night and got wet through, and this morning we were very sorry to find him attacked with fever & ague. We took as much care of him as possible under the circumstances, & towards evening he was rather better.

We spent nearly the whole day huddled round the fire, endeavouring to keep ourselves dry by means of a canopy of mats stretched on the trees above our heads. The rain was the more annoying as it interfered with our drying the meat which was to serve us on our journey home. This we had been doing for some days past. The meat is cut from the Buffalo in broad, thin flaps, principally off the ribs, called by the Canadians, les plats-cotes, and to dry it a kind of frame is built of poles in the shape of a hut, or tent, on which the meat is stretched in layers like the roofing of a house, and exposed to the sun. A slow fire is kept burning inside the hut & the meat being turned 3 or 4 times during the day, soon becomes quite dried & is in that state perfectly fit for eating, altho it is preferable for soup, or boiled, which takes away a slight leatheriness which it possesses in its dry state.

During the afternoon, while we were sitting round the fire, a large eagle came soaring over & lighted on a sandbank in the river, about 40 yards from us. Vansittart loaded his gun & taking a shot at him, disabled him so that he was easily caught. We did not know how to keep him alive, however, so we killed him & Vansittart, Henry & I took it by turns to skin him as the former wished to preserve the skin. It was a ring-tailed eagle* which is the young of the Golden Eagle at 2 years old, and he measured about 7 feet from tip to tip. We heard the wolves howling round the camp all night, which kept the dogs very restless. The howl of a wolf is not like that of a dog, being a shrill yapping scream, very wild & melancholy as it came borne across the Prairie in the intervals between the gusts of wind.

[16th]. Provost & the Canadians had managed to mend the broken wheel yesterday in a very ingenious manner. They put in some new sound spokes of hickory and then bound the whole together, inside & out, all around the spokes & tire, with strips of raw Buffalo hide, which they put on wet, & which when it dried became almost as hard as iron, and quite tough enough to bear going over the prairie grass without injury.

The hide of the Buffalo, when stripped of the hair, is very

*Fairhome's note: Falco Fulvus (Wilson) who believed it to be a distinct species, but Tamminck, Selby and others have decidedly proved it to be the young of the Golden Eagle [Aquila Chrysactos?] at the age of about a year & a half.

thin but exceedingly tough, & will bear a great strain. We made very nice bridles of it, without any bits, merely securing it round the lower jaw of the horse with a bowline knot, & being soft & pliable in the animal's mouth, it kept it moist, a very great advantage on the dry prairies.

As Tabaud said he felt strong enough to bear travelling in one of the waggons, & the day was fine, we made up our minds to commence our return to the settlements. Accordingly about 9 o'clock we set out, & I can truly aver that it was with extreme regret that I, for one, took a last look of the Arkansaw & its solitary groves, and I lingered behind on the heights to take a farewell view of the beautiful panorama below me, beautiful even in its very wildness, with a feeling of melancholy which was heightened by the great improbability of my ever again beholding it. I was soon roused, however, by the impatient snorting of my horse, who not the least participating in my feelings, did not approve of being left behind, & willingly obeyed a light touch of the spur, setting off at a pace which soon brought me up with the others.

In the afternoon, when within 3 miles of where we were to camp, we found a dozen or two of old Bulls scattered about over the Prairie. We all went away after them, & had very good fun for about an hour. Windham & I went together after 2, one of which we killed. He was a monster, & I should have liked much to have brought away his head, but it would have half filled one of the waggons. Presently we came up to Warre who had wounded a Bull which was at bay, with Warre's large dog flying at him very gallantly till the Bull began to show fight, when he was shot. We killed altogether 9 or 10 of them, and it was a stirring sight to see the Buffalo scattered all over the plain, with horsemen riding after them in all directions, shots fired, & Buffalo tumbling over, or savagely charging at their pursuers every moment.

After passing through a large & very wet marsh swarming with ducks, geese & teal, which we saw by the light of the moon, we arrived about 8 o'clock at a creek with a few scattered bushes about it where the camp had been formed. The night came on wet & drizzling & we were very uncomfortable, and were also much displeased at finding that part of our sugar had been stolen by some of the men, but who we could not make out. It was not the loss of the sugar, but the dishonesty of the thief that annoyed us; & moreover it caused some bickering among the Canadians as the guilty party would not confess. As it was Henry who made the complaint, one or two of them accused him, but he proved his innocence most satisfactorily. We found that as they had already had some quarrel with him, & dared not while with us, venture to come to blows, one or two of them had agreed to wait till we arrived at St. Louis, when they would pay off old scores, knowing that there, he being a slave, would not dare to retaliate on them, for any slave who strikes a white man is subject to the most summary punishment. Poor Henry seemed deeply sensible of the degrading distinction drawn in such a case by the laws between black & white men.

We found this creek was merely a part of Cow Creek, lower down than our two former camps on it, & we named this place Ridley Camp.

[17th]. On starting this morning the ox waggon was upset in crossing the creek, which delayed us a short time, but no damage was done, and we were soon en route again. In the middle of the day, when I was behind with the waggons, I saw a large herd of Elk about ½ a mile west of the trail, and was much provoked at finding that Cendre was in front some distance so that I could not go after them, as my poney was not fast enough. As near as I could guess, there appeared to be 90 or 100 of them, and noble animals they seemed, with

immense horns. They looked exactly like a herd of red deer except that their horns are about 3 times as large as any stag's, altho otherwise precisely similar in shape & branches.

We arrived about 5 o'clock at Snow Camp without any adventure, except that Warre & Ridley found an ox wandering about the Prairie & drove him before them into the camp. He had most likely been left behind from weakness by some former party of voyageurs and was in wretched condition. There were an immense number of wild geese on the open flat where we had camped on the 1st, but we did not succeed in getting any, tho Warre, Vansittart & I stalked them on our hands & knees for 2 or 300 yards. The weather continued very fine & sunny during the daytime, but the nights were beginning to get cold.

[18th]. The whole night we were disturbed by the melancholy howling of a number of wolves, one of which ventured actually into the camp, attracted probably by the smell of some of the Buffalo meat which we laid out to dry last night. Windham sallied out upon him with his bow & arrows & took a shot at him by the light of the moon, but missed him.

This morning we started early and after a rather cold ride of 8 hours, arrived at our former camping ground on the Little Arkansaw. Just as we approached it, two Bulls were galloping up the opposite rise, and Ridley going off in chase, very soon shot one, & brought in some of the meat.

We were much amused by the figure Greenwood had made of himself during the last 2 days. He wore very nice white leather hunting breeches, and long yellow Canadian boots up to the middle of the thigh, a pea jacket, and over all, a handsome flowered silk padded French dressing gown, which streamed after him in the breeze in the most picturesque manner as he cantered over the Prairie.

Tabaud had now nearly recovered; and we were glad to be

relieved this evening from our doubts about the sugar stealer by discovering that the Negro driver of the ox waggon was the chief culprit, and Pierre had used the sugar, knowing the same to be stolen. They received a long lecture from Windham and were put in Coventry[83] for some time by the other men, & the Negro was threatened with a severe flogging if he transgressed again, which however, was only a threat which we of course never intended carrying into execution, altho as we had a perfect right to do so, having hired him from his master, it answered as a check upon his propensities. He bore a very bad character & had run away several times from his master & lived with the Indians, & was one of the worst looking specimens I ever saw.

[19th]. We took a supply of wood with us today and late in the evening arrived at the creek where we had camped on the 28th of September. During the middle of the day Greenwood, Windham & I rode after 4 bulls, which we observed a little way off the trail. Greenwood & I each shot one, and Windham had a fine gallop after another, shooting at him with his bow and arrows, but wounding him twice, he was obliged to finish him with his gun.

The frost appeared now to have regularly set in & it was astonishing to observe the difference that the 2 last frosty nights made on the appearance of the horses. Their coats were all staring and they did not look like the same animals we had with us 3 weeks before at this place. Old Cendre and Windham's large chesnut were the only ones that seemed to be utterly indifferent to the weather.

[20th]. We had a dreary ride to Cotton wood Creek, which we reached late, and camped in our old ground. During the day we shot a few prairie hen, some of them close to

[83] A state of exclusion, or banishment: ostracism.

the camp. The weather was getting quite wintry, but with fine sunny days, and we no longer saw the vast flocks of wild fowl going Southwards. The mules & oxen were beginning to get very much fagged at the end of the day, & the latter suffered a good deal in their feet as we had not had time to get them shod, as is the usual custom of the voyageur, before we left Westport.

[21st]. Proceeded to Silver Spring, or Misery Camp, carrying our fuel with us. When in the buffalo country it does not so much signify whether you have wood or not at the camping ground: at least it then becomes a luxury, for the dry dung of the Buffalo forms a tolerable substitute with which you can make a fire sufficient for all culinary purposes, if not for warmth.

Henry reported this evening that the supply of flour was in such a flourishing state that till our arrival in Westport we sh[d] be treated to a double supply of bread, an intimation that was received with 3 cheers.

Our baking was very simple: some flour & water was made into a leathery paste, with salt, quant-duff, rolled out & cut into cakes about the size of a plate, & an inch thick. These were then placed upon a poela or plate of iron which was covered over with another, and put upon some hot coals for a short time, & the result was a very tolerable kind of scone, rather heavy, but very good travelling bread.

[22nd]. Started early and arrived about 6 o'clock at a creek with a pretty thick fringe of wood down its banks. We had seen during the latter part of the journey a remarkable appearance in the Eastern horizon, like a faint glare all along it. During supper Windham observed a smell of burning, and a few light cinders fell about the camp, and presently we remarked that the luminous appearance in the east had very much augmented.

There being a little hill in front of us, we could not see distinctly what caused it, but Windham & Provost having consulted together, agreed that it must proceed from a Prairie Fire which, however, was a long way off. About 8 o'clock the smell of burning, & the glare, having materially increased, Windham & I walked up to the top of the hill when a spectacle presented itself to us, the most grand that can well be conceived. The whole horizon from North to South was one wall of fire, blazing up in some places to a great height, at others merely smouldering in the grass. It was at least 8 miles off, but the wind seemed to set in our direction, so we instantly returned to warn Provost to take measures to preserve the camp. We were in a corner, as it were, on the bank of the stream with a good deal of brush wood running up on our left, and the ground sloping up gradually from the creek to the top of the hill. Provost, on looking at the fire, said that it would not harm us, "ce n'est rien - le vent change" [it's nothing, the wind changes], in short, he would do nothing.[84] In about 20 minutes however, it began to approach so near that there was no time to be lost, and all hands were immediately employed in burning a kind of road across the face of the hill, so as to stop the fire at that part.

A more picturesque scene could hardly be imagined. The night was very dark, but as far as the eye could reach, all across the horizon in front of us, about 4 miles off, was a broad, bright, lurid glace of fire with a thick canopy of smoke hanging over it, whose fantastic wreaths, as they curled in the breeze, were tinged with the red reflection of the flames. Even at that distance we could hear the crackling and rushing of the fire which, as it advanced, caused a strong wind &

[84]Warre wrote, of Provost's comments, "Provost assures us that he has seen many fires, but seldom one that rages with greater fury." Warre placed the party about ten miles west of Council Grove on the night of the fire, and noted they had been seeing the smoke for two days. 75-6.

every now & then a brighter flame would shoot high up into the black cloud of smoke over the top of the hill, illuminating for an instant our tents & waggons in the dark hollow, & giving a momentary glimpse of the horses which were picketed on the side of the rise, on the crest of which the figures of the men engaged in lighting the opposition fire (which as it became too extended they beat down with blankets, only suffering it to burn a space about 12 feet broad right across the line of the advancing conflagration) stood out in strong relief against the glowing wall of light beyond them. As they ran about, tossing their arms & waving the blankets & little torches of lighted grass, they looked in the distance like demons rather than men. We had no time to think of the picturesque, however, for every moment from Provost's obstinacy in neglecting to take precautions in time, became more pregnant with danger, and by the time they had burnt as much as would only about half cover the camp, the fire was raging in the bottom at the other side of the hill. I ran up for an instant to the top & I shall never forget the scene: altho still half a mile off, the fire seemed close to me, and the heat & smoke were almost intolerable, while the dazzling brightness of the flames made it painful to look at them.

They were in three lines nearly parallel, the first of which was just below me, burning with a rushing noise & crackling as it caught the dry grass that gave an idea of *total destruction* which it is impossible to convey, & stretched away over hill & dale for 12 or 14 miles on each side of me, lighting up the sides of the hills & the little groves of wood far away. The two lines in rear were not so connected and seemed rather to be licking up any little spot of grass which had escaped at first.

Every now & then a prairie hen would whirr past, flying in a wild, uncertain manner as if fear had almost deprived them of the use of their wings, while all the songsters of the grove were wheeling about among the trees, uttering the most expressive cries of alarm, & the melancholy hooting of several owls & wailing yell of the wolves, together with the shouts & cries of the men, almost drowned occasionally by the roaring of the flames, added to the savage grandeur of the scene, & one could have fancied the end of all things was at hand.

On returning to the camp I found all hands cutting the lassos of the horses & mules, some of which gallopped off instantly into the river, where they remained standing till the hurricane of flame had passed over. The others, seemingly trusting themselves instinctively more to man than to their own energies in such an emergency, followed us up to the space which we had burnt and remained quietly there, trembling indeed, but without any effort to escape. By the time the animals were collected in this spot the fire was blazing on the top of the hill & we all rushed away with blankets to arrest its progress, if possible, at the part which we had left unguarded. All our efforts would have been in vain, however, & our tents and everything else must have been consumed, but that just at that weak point the grass suddenly became thin & scanty, with much stoney ground, and we had the satisfaction of seeing the flames stopped there and turned off to the Northward along the edge of the brushwood. It was really terrific to be, as we were when trying to beat it down, in the very middle of the blaze (which after all was so narrow that where the flames were not high you could jump across it) and indeed Warre & I were very nearly suffocated by the smoke and heat, & as soon as we perceived the fire turn off we returned to the camp & horses. Henry & Windham succeeded in extinguishing a few flakes of flame which caught the grass near the waggons, and then all real danger was over, but the sight of the three lines of fire stretching up the rising grounds behind the camp, just like the advance of a vast army was magnificent, and it was still more extraordinary to watch the manner in which the fire passed itself on, as it were, over the tops of the highest trees to the height of at least 40 or 50 feet.

Just as the first division had reached the top of the hill we were horrified to perceive the ox waggon (which had come on very slowly, the oxen being knocked up) halted within a few yards of it, and from the glare of the light we could almost see the eyes of the poor animals, who all lay down as the flames approached them. The grass being very high just there, we gave them all up for lost, & were just preparing to go to the assistance of the drivers when we observed the flames suddenly divide, & passing by the waggon, unite again behind it & pursue their devastating course. We learnt, when the waggon came into the camp, that there was providentially a bare spot just where the driver stopped, without which the waggon & oxen must have been destroyed, as there was a cask of gunpowder in it which could hardly have escaped the fire.

As soon as the danger was over, the horses that had gone into the river came cantering back & the whole encampment resumed its usual appearance. We were very sorry to find one of the mules and a poney of Windham's had got severely burnt by some accident, & we were obliged to give corn to all the beasts, there being of course, not a blade of grass left.

The whole scene altogether lasted about 2 hours, and I cannot conceive anything more awfully grand. The extraordinary rushing & crackling sound of the flames was one of most terrific parts of it, and when one considers that the grass is nowhere more than 5 or 6 feet high, it is difficult to imagine how the flame blazes up to such a vast height as it did. The contrast presented 2 hours afterward was most striking. Instead of the brilliant glare of the fire & lurid appearance of the sky, there reigned an impenetrable darkness, earth & sky being alike shrouded in a black gloom, which could almost be felt. Not a star was to be seen, & the air retained a suffocating sulphureous smell as if Satan himself had passed over the earth. We could not distinguish objects at 10 paces distance & were right glad when a fresh breeze came gently breathing over the Prairie, dissipating the murky vapours still hanging in the atmosphere, & disclosing a fine starlit sky, and a sharpish frost relieved us inexpressibly from the close, choking feeling we had experienced for some hours before. The voyageurs all declared they had hardly ever beheld so tremendous a prairie fire, either in height or extent, and it came on at an astonishing pace, going at least 5 miles an hour, & bringing with it a strong gale of wind, for otherwise the night was quite calm, both before & after it had passed over.

[23rd]. What a scene we beheld from our camp this morning! Instead of the waving yellow grass that covered the ground for miles in every direction last night, a vast sea of rolling prairie lay extended before us, all black as night: in vain the eye sought for some green spot on which to rest. The devastating storm of fire which had swept over the whole region had left the surface bare of a single blade of herbage, and the only objects which arrested one's glance, as it wandered over the blackened, and in many places still smoking, wastes of prairie, were the stones on the sides of the hills and numbers of immense elk horns, which had been cast at different periods & which now, exposed to view, & whitened by time & the action of former fires, were glistening in the rays of a bright morning sun, to whose enlivening beams shining clear thro' the frosty air, the eye turned with pleasure from the dreary black landscape below.

While we were at breakfast we were surprised by the entrance of an Indian into the camp who, seating himself quietly by our fire, proceeded to light his pipe. He was a tall handsome fellow, with strong marked features & high cheek bones, fine roman nose, & black gleaming eyes. His head was shaved, all but the chivalrous scalp-lock, which hung down behind, and he wore metasses, or leggings, of dressed deer-skin, which were attached to a belt round his waist, to which were hung his knife, a pouch for tobacco, & a little instrument of wood for pulling out any superfluous hairs from his face & beard. Over his shoulders a blanket was carelessly thrown, which was confined behind by the belt, thus enabling him to throw it off his shoulders in an instant, so as to have his arms free. Deerskin moccassins and a long heavy rifle completed his equipment, & he certainly quite came up to my beau ideal of the North American Indian, as far as his appearance went. He gave us to understand that he was Konza, belonging to a party then on its way from the villages to the Buffalo country for the winter hunting.

We gave him some breakfast for which he seemed very thankful as, from what we could make out, his people were not very well supplied with meat. None of our men understanding the Konza language, our communication was principally carried on by signs.

After breakfast we packed our "butin" & leaving some tobacco & dried Buffalo meat with our Konza friend, we resumed our journey. It was dreary beyond description, being for 17 or 18 miles over the burnt prairie, and every step our horses took sent up a little cloud of dust and ashes. I picked up a few of the elk horns & fixed them to my saddle, but they seemed very rotten, and the least jerk broke off the points of the tynes. They are certainly the finest horns I know, being generally from 4 to 5 feet long, with immense branches. I believe the prairie Elk to be identical with the wapiti, altho I have heard some hunters say that the latter is confined to the country about the Red River, & near Hudson's Bay. The horns, at all events, seem to be precisely the same, but I was not near enough to the Elk I saw to be enabled to say whether the resemblance extends to the rest of the animal. If one may judge by the numbers of these horns that are found on the burnt prairie, the Elk must have been at one time very numerous in these parts—one could often see 20 or 30 of them at a time from the trail, but the Elk themselves are very rarely seen now as near the settlements as Council Grove.

In the afternoon we passed several parties of Indians, all Konzas. The men were equipped much the same as the one I have before mentioned and were mostly mounted on their small hardy little horses. They straggled about the line of march while the women and children, many of them walking, kept together, with the horses carrying their light camping apparatus, which consisted of little more than the poles for their huts (difficult things to be got sometimes on the prairie, & which were consequently taken good care of), a few simple cooking utensils, & some sacks of maize, & perhaps a little flour.

The dress of the women differed very little from that of the men except that their metasses were generally of blue or scarlet cloth, gaily worked in beads or dyed porcupine quills, and that instead of the loose blanket, most of them had a large piece of blue cloth wound round the body, while a few wore a kind of jacket underneath. Their hair, instead of being cut off like that of the men, hung in thick black masses on their ears & shoulders. A few of the younger ones were pleasing looking, but none pretty, but they all had large dark gleaming eyes & beautiful teeth. One of the most striking peculiarities about these Indians is the strong likeness that they all bear to one another: it takes some little time to get accustomed to their countenances before one can distinguish them. I never saw or heard of a deformed Indian, indeed, I believe that all children born with any physical defect are immediately made away with. The scourge of the prairie tribes, the much dreaded small-pox, had this season made great ravages among this tribe and others along the frontier, and several of those we saw looked as if still suffering from the remains of it.

They all made anxious inquiries about the Buffalo, and appeared surprised & pleased to hear that we had found them so near the settlements. I did not observe any bows among them, except in the hands of some of the boys, who are astonishingly dextrous in the use of them.

About 4 o'clock we arrived at our old quarters at Council Grove, but the fire having destroyed all the pasture, we were obliged to camp in the grove itself where the horses got plenty of peavine & tolerable grass. We found a large party of Konzas just breaking up their camp, and about an hour after we got in they all left the grove except 3 or 4 men who remained with us, I am afraid, in the hope of stealing something. However they sat very quietly near the fire, smoking their pipes & accepting with thankfulness whatever we gave them, but we were not very profuse in our hospitality, as there would have been no end to it if they had found us very accommodating. They were much gratified with a large bowl of soup in which there was some Mexican garlic sauce, but did not approve of pepper. We kept a watchful eye upon them & the horses, which are always the most irresistible temptation to a Prairie Indian, but late in the evening they left us to join their own party. On meeting the Indians they always shake hands, saying in an emphatic manner, "Howgh! Howgh!" an expression which they make use of on every occasion. We observed in this party a young girl of very fair complexion, with light hair, but could not discover what her history was She was most probably a half breed however, or had perhaps been kidnapped from the settlements.

[24th]. We remained at Council Grove this day, spending our time in shooting &c, but from the numbers of Indians that had been encamped there during the past week, we had much difficulty in getting as many turkeys as would supply us with fresh meat. Two or three parties of Konzas & Shawanees passed thro' during the day, and there were encampments of them all about the grove, but they did not give us any trouble.

[25th]. We left the grove this morning, the weather still continuing fine. The whole country was a black waste, which made one melancholy even to ride over, and a cold wind whistled cheerlessly over it like the parting sighs of the Grand Prairie at our departure.

About 5 o'clock we arrived at 112 Mile Creek and encamped in the middle of the wood. Greenwood & Henry strolled up to our old encampment on the chance of recovering the pin which the former had lost on the 23rd. of Sept., and much to our surprize Henry did find it, for the grass being all burnt away, his very quick eye was soon attracted by the shining gold, which after being exposed for a month to all the elements, was not even discoloured.

Windham, who had remained behind at Council Grove to shoot, came in at dinner time with 5 turkeys, which at an average of 20 lbs. each was a pretty good bag for one day.

[26th]. We proceeded today to the Great Neosho, where we arrived late. There was a desolate grandeur in these vast blackened plains, which altho very striking at first, became monotonous and dismal to a painful degree after a few days travelling over them, and I think that more than one of us looked forward at this time with pleasure to entering again within the pale of civilisation.

Our horses and mules too, being of necessity stinted in their food, began to show more bone & less spirit than heretofore: and of all disheartening things to men in our position, none is more so than to perceive the animals that have been your companions for so long succumbing under the spare diet, and especially the cold nights to which ours had been exposed for the last few days. Two of these cold frosty nights will tell more on a horse's condition & spirits than weeks of hard work.

[27th]. Went to the lesser Neosho. We did not go to our former ground, but proceeded to a grove about 1/2 a mile lower down the Creek, in the middle of which we found some tolerable pasture. Having seen several parties of Indians during the day, mostly Konzas & Shawnees, who bear a worse character than the Delawares, we were rather uneasy about the horses, which were more dispersed than was safe. Soon after dinner some Indians came & seated themselves by our fire. They belonged to a party of Konzas encamped at a little distance, and having treated them with the hospitality invariably practised on the Prairies, we gently intimated to them that their absence would be agreeable, on which they took themselves off. During the night we were a good deal disturbed by the restlessness of the animals, particularly the oxen which, yoked together in pairs, with bells attached to their necks were constantly mooing up & down the woods, as if they were disturbed.

The dogs too gave unequivocal signs that something wrong was going on, but some of us having searched the purlieus of the camp without discovering anything, we took no further notice of their alarm.

[28th]. This morning on mustering the animals, an Indian poney of Warre's was missing. Recollecting our disturbances last night, a party instantly gallopped off towards the Konza camp, but in about ½ an hour returned having found the birds flown. They had however tracked the missing horse, which had been taken thro the thickest part of the grove,

Ground Ash Camp

down a steep bank, & across the river, and his trail was plainly distinguishable going away west. Apparently he had been at full gallop [and] there could be no doubt that the Indians had carried him off.

About 5 in the evening we came in sight of Ground Ash Camp, but between us and it, the whole country was occupied by the enemy, alias a splendid prairie fire. However, by the time it reached us we had got upon a previously burnt spot of ground where we remained very quietly for about ½ an hour, till it had passed us, and then proceeded to the camp. There was not a particle of forage, and barely enough fuel for our fires, so that as the night was cold we were rather uncomfortable: moreover the prairie fire was raging all round us the whole night, which kept us on the alert.

[29th]. The waggons started some little time in advance this morning, and when we began our march we agreed to take a short cut across the prairie and join them at Black Jack Grove. Accordingly, we followed the Ground Ash Creek about 2 miles to the East, and then took a Northerly direction. The prairie was here very little burnt, owing to the swamps & bogs which we crossed in every direction, and we saw several snipes.

Wherever the grass was burnt we found great numbers of elk horns, and I slung 3 or 4 of them to my saddle. My horse did not approve of them at all for, they were no small addition to his burden, besides which the points of the tynes kept irritating his flanks and interfering with his hind legs, as even at that height from the ground they reached within a few inches of it.

After 2 or 3 hours riding we began to think we had lost our way, and accordingly struck off to the N.W., & after another hour came upon the trail and perceived the waggons about a mile ahead of us, skirting the edge of Black Jack Grove. About 4 o'clock we crossed part of the Grove and encamped on the same small stream as on the 17th Sept/r but about 2 miles further West. We had plenty of wood & water and pitched our tents on small bank which sloped down from a thick bush of Black Jack oaks to the creek. There were some prairie hens shot near the camp, which formed an agreeable addition to our dried Buffalo meat. This evening Greenwood, Warre & Paterson, resolved to ride on before us tomorrow morning & get to Westport in one day instead of two, and altho we tried to dissuade Greenwood from it, as a ride of 50 or 60 miles was rather more than a man in his weak condition ought to attempt, yet he said he felt quite equal to it & they made their arrangements accordingly.

[30th]. Greenwood & the others started early after having

amused themselves, while their horses were being prepared, in shooting some of the thousands of prairie hen which were flying about or perched among the trees close to the camp. It was a most extraordinary sight to see the low, thick black jack bushes covered with these birds, like with flocks of starlings, and altho they did not let one get within shot of them on the trees, we picked up a good many as they flew about, and plenty were lying in the grass. I imagine that they collect together in these vast flocks at this season as grouse pack late in the autumn at home, and when the prairies are burnt, they feed principally on berries in the woods. In hard weather they become very tame and may be seen in winter perched in hundreds on the stooks in farms on the outskirts of the settlements, when they may be shot like sparrows on a hedge.

We did not raise camp till 12 o'clock, as Henry was employed in baking for tonight, there being very little wood at Elm Grove where we intended to camp. We were glad to see, as we advanced, that the mules & oxen appeared to begin to know where they were, and they stepped out with such good will that by the time we arrived at Elm Grove it was still early, and we pushed on at once for Round Grove.

Windham found during the day that he had forgotten his handsome Indian belt, with a beautiful powder horn & shot pouch attached to it, at Black Jack Grove, but it was then too late to go back for it, and meeting a very handsome young Delaware near Elm Grove, he explained to him whereabouts it was & told him to keep it if he could find it, which we afterward heard he did. We met this day several parties of Indians: indeed, as we were now in the direct line from the villages to the hunting grounds, we were constantly in sight of some of them.

About 6 in the evening we arrived at Round Grove where we had a very comfortable camp. It was not without regret that we remembered that this was our last night on the Prairies & I felt quite sorry at the idea of parting with my horses. Our men also seemed to be sorry at so soon quitting their "*bourgeois*" as they called us: a delicate distinction as we were not exactly their equals, & they did not look on us quite as their masters. This term, however, is applied by all Canadians to persons whom they accompany as guides, hunters, &c. & is equivalent to "governor" as used by English gamekeepers, &c.

The Return
Westport to St. Louis

[31st]. We started early, & had a very pleasant ride into Westport. I had not seen this part of our journey, having lost my way when going to Round Grove before from Westport. All the country bordering on the settlements is very pretty, being rather hilly and beautifully wooded, with small bright streams meandering thro the groves. Every now & then you pass through some neat Indian farm embosomed among immense hickory & cotton wood trees. The farms at this season, however, are nearly all deserted, their dusky inhabitants being many miles away to the West on their winter hunt, to return again in Spring loaded with Buffalo meat & hides & to renew their farming occupations till the next Fall.

We did not enter Westport through Parker's farm, but went by a most lovely forest path at the back of it, through rich dark groves which reminded me of an English pheasant preserve, except that no English park could show the brilliant colouring of these woods or the neat, tidily dressed & well mounted squaws whom we met cantering along the winding paths occasionally, on their way home from Westport. We found old Mynheer Vogel and his wife in great force and as hospitable as ever.

The beasts were all turned into a field opposite his house, in the middle of the village, where they were soon surrounded by the motley crew of idlers always to be seen lounging about an American frontier village, who inspected them minutely in the view of getting some good bargains out of the

Britishers. The mules & oxen looked better than we expected, but some of the horses were reduced to a wretched condition.

Greenwood, Warre, & Paterson had sold most of theirs for a mere trifle, & I resolved to wait till I arrived at Independence, where I hoped to find a better market. The men were very soon surrounded by a crowd, who took them to the bar of the tavern & treated them, & by the time they had told all their adventures to their admiring auditors they were quite unfit for duty and we had to pitch our tents ourselves.

[Nov/r. 1st]. We left Westport today after having got rid of all our horses except mine & a poney of Windham's. The mules for the waggons we also retained, selling all the others tolerably well. Herr Vogel took a very affectionate leave of us, and well he might for he had made a very good sum by us altogether. However as such a chance comes but rarely in his way, we did not grudge him his gains. We had a most beautiful ride to Independence through splendid forests and arrived there about 4 o'clock. We found that a steamer had gone up, and was to return tomorrow, so Greenwood proceeded immediately down to the Independence landing on the Missouri, about 4 miles from the town. We resolved to follow in the morning, as she was not expected down till 12 o'clock: and we had a very comfortable camp in a field near the town.

Independence is quite a small place, entirely built of wood, with the exception of the church and a few of the principal houses. The whole place was in a ferment, the next day being the first of the elections, and as parties ran high just then (it being the grand contest between General Harrison & Mr. Van Buren for the Presidency) a close contest was expected. We shot 2 or 3 prairie hen which came and perched on the trees close to the camp, and within 1/4 mile of the town.

[2nd]. We raised camp about 9 o'clock and went into Independence, which was crowded with free & *Independent* Electors. Our appearance caused a great sensation, especially when it became known, by means of the crier, that all our goods & chattels were immediately to be put up to auction, which we found would be the readiest way of getting rid of them. Accordingly, through the means of the district auctioneer, I had the pleasure of seeing my 2 horses sold for 45 dollars! We could get nothing like a fair bid for our mules & waggons, so they were made over to Provost for about 280 dollars as part payment of his wages.[85]

The scene was rather an interesting one from the variety of character & dress exhibited in the crowd of bystanders. The sharp-faced Yankee from the East with his high, pale forehead & pawkie[86] deep set eyes & lank, loose, yet muscular form; the pale Virginian or Carolina man with jet black eyes & hair; the bluff, honest looking Kentuckian, were mingling among the throng of Germans, Dutch, Frenchmen, negroes, Spaniards from Santa Fe, and all the heterogeneous inhabitants who form the population of the Western border towns: nor were Indians from the frontier tribes wanting to complete the picture.

The all-engrossing topic of conversation was the approaching election & wherever you turned your ear caught such expressions as "Log-cabin," "hard cider," "Van Buren," "Old Harrison," &c. &c. and "dollar," which last word is constantly in the mouths of all Americans. You cannot listen to a group of men for a few minutes without hearing it repeated more than once.

[85]Warre differs somewhat in his view. "We at once put up all the mules &c. to auction then (though we had several offers the night before) no one bid! The wily Yankees knew how we were pressed for time, and hoped to get our waggons and beasts for a song at the last moment by delaying us. Not to be so done, however, we handed over the lot to our head man in lieu of wages, though nearly double what he was entitled to..." 85.

[86]Pawkie: British dialect meaning shrewd, cunning, or crafty.

About 11 o'clock, having got rid of all our heavy baggage, we set out in a pair-horse waggon for Independence landing having first, however, taken leave of Patterson, who having his own horse & waggon which he had left here on his way up, intended going to St. Louis by land. The landing is 4 miles from the town, but the road being very rough through a thick forest, we were an hour and a half going there. On arriving we were astonished to hear from the squatter living there that the steamer had returned from Westport last night and Greenwood had gone down in her, but they expected another one up in the course of the day. At this time the steamer's movements are very uncertain for as the river may within a few days become unnavigable from the setting in of the frost, the steam boat proprietors will not run the risk of their boats being detained all the winter so high up as this, as occasionally has happened.

We were thus, as the Yankees say, in a fix, but as we saw no use in returning to Independence, we unpacked our baggage and sent back the waggon, and amused ourselves as we best could all the morning.

Henry, with old Provost and the other men came down in the course of the day, & we had our dinner &c just as usual.

The landing was at a very romantic spot. The banks rose high up, with a good deal of wood; and some large precipitous rocks overhung it. Under these was the cottage of the only inhabitant of the place, who with his wife and family, seemed very comfortable, and supplied us with bread, milk, &c. We shot a few squirrels, but did not go far from the river. Towards 3 o'clock we heard 2 hounds giving tongue most melodiously in the thick woods above us, and presently a fine doe came bounding down the steep bank, and plunging 15 or 20 feet down into the river close to us, swam across, and landing on a low sandbank, trotted across it into the opposite woods.

In a few minutes 2 noble hounds came on her trail, and without a moment's hesitation dashed into the broad stream, & after some beautiful hunting on the sandbank (having landed much lower down than the deer) they took up the scent, & making the whole valley re echo with their deep notes they were soon lost to view in the forest. They were large, heavy dogs, of the old English Southern breed with deep chests and immense dew laps, & I never heard finer voices.

The Missouri was here about 1/4 of a mile broad, & the whole scene was as pretty a bit of woodland Romance as I ever saw. As the afternoon wore on without any steam boat making its appearance, we took counsel with the Canadians and at length it was resolved that we should buy a large flat bottomed scow that was lying there, belonging to the squatter, and accompanied by Henry and any of the other men who would go, should float down the Missouri till we should fall in with a steamer, or if necessary, even down to St. Louis. Tabaud (to his honour be it said) was the only one of the Canadians who volunteered to go with us. I fancy Provost had engaged them to assist him in taking down the waggons to St. Louis.[87] We soon bought the scow for 50 dollars. She was a good large craft, fit to hold 10 or 12 men, & having made a bed of clay & gravel near one end for a fire place, and arranged all our bedding &c. as conveniently as possible, we took a very friendly leave of Provost and the other Canadians and embarked. Henry and Windham each took an oar, Tabaud went to the helm, and away we went about 5 o'clock of as lovely an evening as we could have wished for, down the broad bosom of the Missouri.

We had laid in a supply of flour, butter, &c, from the cot-

[87]Warre again differs in some detail from Fairholme's journal. Warre indicates the men were offered continued employment to row the scow; however, they had been paid off for their prairie service, and were then so full of both liquor and cash that they scorned the offer. They had bought a light canoe for their own transportation downriver. Both parties set off downriver together, but the scow had outdistanced the canoe by the second day. 86.

tage, and the squatter killed a pig, of which we took half, so that we were well provisioned, and I never enjoyed a more complete feeling of independence than then. The water was calm as a mirror, with all the gorgeous colors of an American sunset reflected in it, while from the high banks on each side of us, clothed in forest, not a sound disturbed the still evening air, and Tabaud's voice, as he now & then chanted forth the plaintive refrain of some Canadian boat song, was echoed across the glassy water from the broken precipices forming the picturesque boundaries of the river.

Excepting these occasional snatches of melody, the most perfect & delicious silence reigned over the lonely woods. I always found something peculiarly soothing and melancholy in a fine Autumn evening in America. The fading colours of the trees, the occasional cracking of a decayed branch, the rustling of the falling leaves, the wild cry of the Whip poor Will, and even the chatter of some dissipated squirrel retiring to rest later than his more sober companions, give an idea of peace & repose to the mind which is difficult to express, and one's thoughts involuntarily take a turn of melancholy, elevating them above the common drudgery of life. On this evening in particular I took extreme pleasure in Tabaud's mournful airs, and in listening to the quiet gurgling of the water as we rapidly glided down the stream. We continued our voyage till it became too dark to see to steer, and then running the scow into a little creek, we made her fast and lighting a fire on the bank resigned ourselves to repose.

[3rd. 4th. & 5th]. We were still on the Missouri during all these days, stopping at night and starting at 4 or 5 o'clock in the morning.

The weather was quite beautiful: in fact we were so lucky as to have just commenced our voyage as the "Indian Summer," as it is called, had set in, and I do not know a more perfectly enjoyable season than the few days of fine weather before the hard winter, which go by that name. The sun during the day was just warm enough to be pleasant, and the nights were not too cold.

The navigation of the river in many places was very intricate owing to the quantities of sand & mud banks on which we constantly got aground, and not less so, to the immense snags & sawyers which interrupt the course of the stream in every direction, causing eddies & whirlpools which to a flat bottomed boat like our ark were very dangerous. Tabaud however, knew them well, and was an excellent steersman.

We had capital opportunities for shooting, and on one island where we landed to get a shot at some wild turkies we saw on the bank, we found 8 deer in about as many minutes. During the day we generally stopped at any house near the river, where we were sure to find plenty of venison, beautiful honey, milk, and such other provisions as we required to replenish our stock.

Every mud or sand bank was covered with wild fowl, which however were very difficult to shoot. There was an inexpressible charm to most of us in this independent kind of life although it must be confessed that as we approached nearer to civilization occasional visions of comfortable Hotels, warm baths, &c would present themselves to us.

[6th]. We arrived about 4 o'clock at Glasgow, a small place on the left bank of the river, at which, as a steamer was expected up that day, I resolved to stop, for the thick fogs which prevail in the valley of the Missouri at this season in the early morning had brought on a slight relapse of my ague, and I did not feel equal to going down to St. Louis in the scow. Accordingly, I went up to the small Inn while the others went on in the boat, but a most tremendous thunderstorm coming on just after they had set out, they only went about

1/2 a mile down when they landed & encamped in a wood. There were not above 70 or 80 houses in the whole place, & the population seemed very primitive.

I was much amused during and after dinner with some farmers who had come in from a short distance. Their manners were quite new even to me, who had then seen something of the Men of the West, but they were by no means vulgarly disagreeable, altho rough & hearty.

In the evening a small steamer arrived and went up, to return in the morning; and as the rest of our party had changed their plans, we sold the scow, after some trouble, for 30 dollars, and prepared to go down to St. Louis by steamer, all together.

[7th]. About 11 o'clock we embarked in the steamer, which returned early this morning. We were on the river all day, and stopped in the evening for a few hours till the moon rose, it being otherwise too dark to permit us to proceed in safety through this dangerous navigation.

While thus detained, a negro came on board with some opossums, which he had just taken in a tree not far off, and as he said there were more, we went out for a short time & got two by applying damp straw, lighted, to a hole in the tree. The smoke drives them out & they are thus easily secured at the mouth of the hole. I bought one of them alive from him, and got a box where he seemed to be very comfortable. They are nice pets and very clean in their habits.

[8th]. On the river all day and arrived about sunset at St. Charles, a small town near the junction of the Missouri & Mississippi, where we remained for the night on account of the dangerous shoals in this part of the stream.

[9th]. Arrived at St. Louis about 10 o'clock A.M. after having been absent 2 months & 17 days. We immediately proceeded to the Hotel, where we were very sorry to find

Greenwood confined to his bed, having been very ill ever since his arrival about 6 days ago. However he was much better today, and as a steamer was to start for Pittsburgh next day, and he thought himself equal to the journey, we arranged to go by her.

We very soon settled all our affairs and found most of our baggage &c all right, except a coat & one or 2 other things of mine which were absent without leave, and could not be found. We spent the day in walking about the town and among other things saw the splendid collection of fossils which has been made here by a German named Koch. It was here that I first saw the magnificent fossil skeleton which is now (1843) in London, and which Mr. Koch was then putting together in the theatre. He calls it the Missourean, and it is the largest known skeleton, being 15 feet in height and upwards of 30 feet long, and appears to be altogether a new species of Elephant.[88]

The good people of St. Louis had resolved to celebrate our return by giving us a Ball, but several circumstances rendered it impossible for us to avail ourselves of their kind & hospitable intentions, so we left them our best thanks & good wishes. I got thro Henry a very nice box for my oppossum.

[88]Dr. Albert Koch (b. 10 May 1804, d. 28 December 1867) opened a museum in St. Louis in 1836 in which was displayed an eclectic collection of items ranging from Egyptian mummies to wax figures and animal oddities. There were also special, live, shows of ventriloquism and exotic performers. From the description, the museum appeared to be a combination of medicine show, carnival side show, and P.T. Barnum excess. In October, 1838 Koch discovered some animal fossils in Gasconade County, Missouri, and in 1839 discovered more at Sulphur Springs, among them the skull of an animal that was reported to be six times the size of an elephant. Koch gathered his specimens around his primary find, the "Missourium," which he described as "until now a perfectly unknown animal," and in 1840 opened a new museum of natural history. More fossil bones were found in 1840, and were added to the collection in August, and this expanded exhibit is what Fairholme saw in 1840. The museum was closed in 1841, and Koch took the exhibits on the road, starting in New Orleans. MHS *Bulletin*. IV:4, 233-256. McDermott, John Francis. "Dr. Koch's Wonderful Fossils."

The Adventure Ends
Return to Barracks

[10th]. We were much annoyed today by the constant delays of the steamer, which was to have sailed at 12, but did not get away till 5 when, having parted with Ridley (who was going on to make a tour through the West Indies via New Orleans) and taken an affectionate farewell of Henry & Tabaud, we embarked.[89]

I was really sorry at parting with Tabaud who was, without exception, the best Canadian I ever saw, and he poor fellow seemed as much affected with sorrow as we were. Give me a French Canadian to travel with rather than any other men I have seen. Frank, cordial and obliging, they are more companionable in good fortune and more willing & hardworking in difficulties than any other class of men, and they never degenerate into vulgarity, always keeping their proper place.

Mr. Kenneth McKenzie also had all our good wishes, for to no one were we more indebted for kind attentions, & without him we might have had a great deal of trouble at first starting on our expedition. We had a beautiful evening and a very pleasant voyage down the Mississippi till we arrived at the mouth of the Ohio, which we entered at nightfall.

[11th]. I was much grieved this morning to find my poor pet, the opossum, had died during the night, probably from cold, as a careless cabin boy had put the box out on the open deck and the night was frosty. I paid the last honours to his

---

[89]The *Daily Missouri Republican* for 10 November 1840 listed the steamboats Utica and Harrisburg as departing St. Louis for Pittsburgh that day.

remains by giving him a seaman's burial in the muddy waters of the Ohio.

We were on this river the whole day. The scenery was charming, and, excepting that it was much wilder and more wooded, reminded me a good deal of the Moselle & upper Rhine. We stopped at, & passed, several small towns & villages, and in the afternoon remained about an hour at the City of Cincinnati, a large handsome town, which rises off the Ohio, very much as St. Louis does off the Mississippi. There seemed a great deal of business going on, but of course we did not see much of the place. Here we got into a smaller steamer, as the shallowness of the river above Cincinnati at this season would not permit of our going up in the large one.

We began to observe a few large blocks of ice floating down the stream today, showing that the winter had fairly set in higher up the Country. Our new steamer was in such a condition from old age and want of repairs that her Captain refused to take charge of her. The steam exuded from the boilers in every direction, in fact, I believe that was the only thing preserved us from being blown up, for the holes answered as so many safetyvalves.

We all had to undergo an unceasing round of questions about our expedition, one of which invariably was "What did you get for your Buffalo skins?" They never imagined that we could have left 130 skins, worth 3 or 4 dollars each, to rot on the Prairie.

[12th]. At 6 o'clock this morning we arrived at Wheeling, a large town in the very Northernmost corner of Virginia. From hence there is a magnificent road across the Alleghany Mountains to Baltimore called the National Road, which was begun by a Company, & was finished by Government. Our original plan had been to go by the Ohio as far as Pittsburg, about 80 miles higher up, and from thence to Baltimore

by a canal, which is the principal means of conveyance for merchandise &c. to the Southeastern part of the states. But we understood at Wheeling that from the extreme shallowness of the river just now, it was very possible that the steamer might not get as far as Pittsburg, and even if we got there, all travelling on the canal would probably be stopped by the ice. Accordingly we changed our intention and ordered an Extra (Stage Coach) to be ready at 9 o'clock to convey us by the National Road to Frederic, 40 miles on this side of Baltimore.

We got breakfast at the Hotel and about 1/2 past 9 started on our hard journey of about 220 miles. Wheeling is a handsome town, mostly built of stone, and is a bustling commercial place, but we did not see much of it. We had a most delightful day's journey, getting at once into the Alleghanies. I never saw a more beautiful range of Mountains, full of deep dark gorges & ravines thro which the road winds, now under lofty precipices which reminded me of some of the passes of the Black forest, now long a high crest of Mountain, overlooking a vast extent of beautiful country, now thro' some thick primaeval forest, the favourite abode of bears, wolves, deer, and panthers, or *painters* as they are there called.

During a great part of the day we travelled up the Monongehela River, celebrated in America for the Whiskey made along its bank, but we were generally so high above it that we only saw it like a broad sheet of silver winding thro a rich and highly cultivated valley. Every now & then we made a rapid descent at full gallop down some deep gorge, into which at this late season the beams of the sun seldom penetrate, and in which there was always plenty of snow & ice.

The road was as fine as one as I ever saw in England, and the bridges (of which there must be more than 100) are all very handsomely built of stone, and everything is kept in the highest order. We changed horses 2 or 3 times in the course of the day, and travelled at an average pace of 8 miles an hour, very good going in such a mountainous district.

Altogether I never enjoyed a day's journey more and all of us were in high spirits, Exhilarated by the rapid pace we were going, and by the delicious fresh, free air of the mountains, and I only regretted not having time to take some sketches for I never beheld more tempting subjects for the pencil.

Coal of the finest kind is found in immense quantities all through the Alleghanies: and at all the towns along the road they were burning it at about 4/6 a ton. We passed thro a good many small towns very much resembling country towns at home, & altogether the cultivated part was more like England than anything I have yet seen in America. Our turn out w[d] have astonished an English coachman as much as our own appearance would have alarmed an English landlord, for I must say we were rather suspicious looking characters in our Buffalo hunting costumes.

On leaving Union, where we stopped to dine, we had to ascend a very long hill, which Windham & I walked up, keeping in front of the coach, and on arriving at the top, just before getting in, I took a look at the baggage which was tied on behind. It was just as well I did so for some scoundrel had followed us from the town, cut the ropes & stolen Wyndham's two carpet bags and my guncase, which last, as I had my gun in a leather cover inside the coach, was no great loss, being much broken, but Wyndham had a valuable pair of double barreled pistols in one of the bags and all his Buffalo tongues & humps in the other. It was no use at that late hour attempting to recover them, so we refixed the baggage and consoled ourselves with our cigars till we forgot our troubles in sleep.

I believe Wyndham recovered the pistols some months afterwards by means of our application to the State Authorities.

[13th]. I awoke this morning out of such a troubled slumber as one usually gets in a coach, just in time to see the sun rising in all his splendour over a high mountain to our left. The tops of the hills were just tinged with his golden beams, while the deep, dark valleys looked blacker & deeper from the contrast.

We were going down a very steep hill into one of these gorges, and it was rather ticklish work. There had been a slight fall of snow in the night and the horses were going down the steep descent at full speed, slipping & tumbling about in a manner that would have alarmed any but an American Coachman, but our Jehu[90] seemed utterly unconscious of any danger, and we rattled down the smooth road, turning sharp round high precipices on our right, while on the left a very slight swerving of the coach would have sent us down 3 or 400 feet into the rocky bed of a brawling mountain stream, which ran round the base of the mountain.

However we got down safe and during the rest of the day we continued far down this stream whose constant windings opened to our view the most beautiful mountain & woodland scenery. In many places its course was confined for some distance by immense walls of rock, when we had to cross a handsome stone bridge every 4 or 500 yards, according to the turns of the stream. In others it opened into fine rich flat haughs, mostly well cultivated, from the edges of which the mountains rose with a bold slope, beautifully clothed in wood, glowing with all the colours of the rainbow, till on the very summit, where one could only discern a few scattered clumps of birch and mountain ash entirely stripped of their foliage by the cold autumnal winds, to which at that great elevation they were exposed more than their more favoured brethren below.

[90]A Jehu is a fast, reckless driver or coachman: intended as a humorous term.

We changed coaches 2 or 3 times during the day but did not pass any towns, having now reached the highest ridge of the Alleghanies. About 7 in the evening we arrived at the small town of Cumberland where, after many pros & cons, we agreed to sleep, for we were all a good deal knocked up by our rapid 36 hours journey, not having been accustomed to coach travelling for some time past. The Inn was a very good one, and our host a remarkably civil & obliging personage, and a great sportsman withal, and while smoking our cigars before bedtime we heard from him some very interesting details of adventures with bears & panthers in the surrounding forests. Fox & deer hunting are also favourite pursuits, & most of the farmers keep 2 or 3 couple of hounds.

The woods being very open in many places, they often follow the hounds on horseback, & by our host's account it must be very good sport. The farmers, & that class of persons, who with us would be called Cocklairds,[91] are generally well off, and from what we saw of them seem to be an intelligent well-educated set of men, and have very little of the bragging, blustering manners of the Western Yankees.

[14th]. I was awoke this morning by a most musical cry of hounds, & for a moment could not conceive where I was, but as soon as I had dressed the landlord took me down to his stable where he showed me about 15 couple of very nice fox-hounds, well matched and very well bred. He told us that he had received some of them from England, and from them he had raised the pack we saw, which certainly did him great credit.

After breakfast we recommenced our journey, and had a beautiful drive of 43 miles to Frederic, a large town just at the foot of the Alleghanies. We were, of course, descending them all the latter part of the day, and there appeared to be more

[91] In Scotland, a Cocklaird is a small landowner.

cultivation on this side than on the West, although the scenery was by no means so romantic as in the glens and ravines we came thro yesterday.

From Frederick there is a railroad to Baltimore, and one of the trains being on the point of starting just as we arrived, Vansittart & Warre went on in it, while Greenwood, Windham & I remained for the night. We found the Hotel very good & got nice English looking bedrooms.

[15th]. At 9 o'clock this morning we left Frederic in a remarkably comfortable railroad car and had a pleasant journey to Baltimore, where we arrived about 2 o'clock. The country we passed thro was very beautiful and highly cultivated, and we observed some very fine farms and pretty country houses. It was altogether a good deal like an English landscape and the weather was rather warmer than on the Western side of the mountains.

About 4 miles before reaching Baltimore you enter upon a succession of large flat meadows, divided by ditches, and full of fine cattle, and about 1/2 a mile outside the town, having changed our engine for a team of 4 splendid horses, we rattled into the town at a great pace, till we stopped at the railway office, a very handsome mass of building with large yards & covered courts full of cars, & thronged with people.

We soon got a hackney coach and drove through a great part of the town, and along a magnificent line of quays crowded with shipping, and pulled up at the Exchange Hotel, an immense building adjoining the exchange. Here we got very good rooms & an excellent dinner at the Table d' Hote, at which I tasted for the first time the celebrated canvass backed duck,* which certainly is as much superior to any other game I know as Buffalo beef is to any other meat. These birds are found I believe only in the large marshes &

*Fairholme's note: Anas Valisneria (Wilson).

fields of wild rice along the shores of the Chesapeake & Delaware Estuaries; at least I never heard of them any where else. They feed on a kind of weed peculiar to these waters, which gives to them, and to many other kinds of waterfowl that frequent the same localities, a delicacy of flavour which is only approached by the barnacle & other wildfowl that are found in the Bay of Wexford in Ireland.

Baltimore is mostly built of brick, but there are a great many very handsome stone buildings, and it is altogether a noble city. I had not time to see much of it in a short ramble I took after dinner, but I was much struck with the principal streets, which both in size & paving &c are equal to any I ever saw, and the shops are handsome & well lighted up in the evening. The streets were quite thronged with people taking their evening walk, and a very well dressed respectable population they seemed to be.

I had often heard of the beauty of the Baltimore woman, and I was not disappointed in them, for I never saw so many pretty faces before in so short a time. I got a few Books in a shop which I was obliged to enter in self defence, for I had a crowd of boys after me, staring at my glass, which I as usual wore in my eye, and when I came out of the library there was a small crowd anxiously awaiting my reappearance, but I disappointed them by not wearing it. I was rather an uncouth figure in other aspects, for having lost my only coat at St. Louis, my costume consisted of a Canadian cloth grey jacket, made like a groom's, & coming partly over my hips & trowsers of the same, both very old & covered with stains of blood &c. and to crown all, a remarkably smart bran-new hat, so that among all the welldressed people around me I must have appeared as if just caught.

[16th]. Greenwood not being able to start by the early train for Philadelphia, Windham remained with him, but as

I had never been there, & had little time to spare, I left Baltimore at 9 o'clock by railroad. The distance is about 45 or 50 miles and it is a very pleasant journey.

We had to cross a ferry over the Chesapeake Bay, for which purpose a large and peculiarly constructed steamboat is used, having a railroad along its whole length so that the baggage cars have merely to be detached from the train & run along into the boat, and on arriving at the opposite shore are run out again at once on to the railroad: this saves an infinite deal of trouble.

The country is quite flat, and very marshy, the road being formed on an embankment running along the border of the estuary for the greater part of the way. I never saw such ground for duck-shooting, and was tantalized during the whole journey by observing immense flocks of canvass backed & other kinds of ducks swimming about almost within shot of the cars.

The approach to Philadelphia is very beautiful. For some distance before you reach the town you pass through a deep cut in a hill, and on emerging very suddenly from it you behold the whole city stretched out before you, forming a splendid panorama. On the left, above the town, are the celebrated waterworks by which it is supplied with water from the Schuykill, and to the right is the broad estuary of the Delaware, covered with vessels of all sizes, from the light & peaceful pilot boats with their enormous mast & sail, to the lordly 3 decker. We crossed the Schuykill by a very long & handsome bridge, and as at Baltimore, changed our engine for a team of horses, & soon arrived at the large & handsome railway office. I drove immediately to the Mansion house Hotel, which is considered one of the best in the States, and is kept by jovial looking Englishman.

Having no time to lose, I immediately walked out to see

the town, and although I was in some degree prepared to like Philadelphia, I had no idea what a splendid city it is. In fact, I do not know any where so handsome a place. The houses are mostly built of brick, but better than any I ever saw, and from the wide paves, the excellent repair they are kept in, the splendid shops & lofty buildings, the streets struck me as being really magnificent. The extrordinary cleanliness of the city particularly attracts one's admiration. This is occasioned principally by the superabundant supply of water, which is afforded by the Waterworks of the Schuykill, and handsome cast iron pumps are among the most prominent features of the streets.

I strolled about all the evening and about 7 returned to dinner, in which I was joined by a remarkably pleasant gentlemanlike man, a Major in the U.S. Army. The dinners of the Mansion house are proverbially good, and altogether I never was in a better house. Late in the evening Windham & Greenwood arrived and we settled to go to New York by the afternoon train tomorrow.

[17th]. The first thing I went to see this morning was the celebrated Chinese Museum. This magnificent collection was made by a gentleman of Philadelphia named Dunne who, when very young, went out to China, and after some years, having made a large fortune & an immense collection of Chinese curiosities, he embarked for America, sending his property in another ship. On his arrival the first news that greeted him was that this ship had been lost, and after so many years labour he was as poor as when he first began life. Nothing daunted however, he returned to China and succeeded in again amassing a large sum of money, and returned home in safety, bringing with him another museum. He immediately built a handsome edifice to contain it, and it is now open to the public for a small entrance fee, the proceeds

of which he intends to apply to defray the expenses during his life, and at his death the whole is to go to his native city.[92]

You enter an immense hall, of I should think, 70 or 80 feet in length by 40 wide, and about 30 in height, with 2 rows of columns down each side at 15 feet from the wall. These, and the walls and roof, are all beautifully painted in rich blue & gold arabesque work in the Chinese style.

A space of about 14 feet of the upper end of the hall is partitioned off and fronted with glass, forming a kind of separate room. This is divided into 3: the largest division represents a room in a gentleman's house in China, another a shop, & the third a room in the Emperor's palace. These are fitted up most beautifully and correctly, and dispersed among them are several figures the size of life (& so like that one requires to go very close to be certain that they are not real people) all dressed in the costumes appropriate to the inhabitants of each division.

Down the left side of the hall at small intervals are other glass fronted partitions or cases to the number of 8 or 10, such of which contain from 2 to 8 figures, all the size of life, which represent every different class of persons in China, beginning at the poorest labourer, till the last representing the Emperor himself surrounded by some children & ladies of the Court, absolutely dazzles one by the splendour of the dresses & the profusion of jewels.

The richness & texture of the silks, brocades &c. and the

---

[92]Nathan Dunn (1782-1844) went to China as a merchant (perhaps) in early 1818, returning home in 1831. On 20 December 1838 he opened his Chinese Museum, which was said to occupy a room 163 by 70 feet. A catalog of 120 pages entitled *Ten Thousand Chinese Things...with Miscellaneous Remarks upon the Manners, Customs, and Government of the Celestial Empire,* was widely distributed. There is no mention of his having to replace a lost collection, but he was assisted in his collecting in Canton by another Philadelphian, William Whiteman Wood. The museum closed in 1842, and was moved to London. The collection was reported to have been destroyed by fire in Edinburgh. Hummell, Arthur W. "Nathan Dunn." *Quaker History*. Friends Historical Association, Spring, 1970.

fineness of the workmanship of the jewels, gold & silver ornaments &c. quite astonished me. I never saw anything so splendid, and all the figures are so admirably carved and put in such natural attitudes they very materially add to the wonder of the beholder. They were all made in China.

Down the opposite side of the room are similar cases containing every kind of luxury & comfort, while between the pillars are other cases in which one sees all the innumerable fancy articles in ivory, gold, silver &c for which the Chinese are so celebrated. There are also cases full of models of houses, bridges (of which there they have 15 or 20 kinds, some of them of most extraordinary beauty & workmanship), cooking utensils, & surgical instruments of every possible & conceivable variety, and an immense quantity of musical instruments of all kinds, besides China ware in every shape one can imagine, gold, silver & other metal ornaments, a vast & beautiful collection of arms & armour - chairs, tables & other domestic furniture, the beauty of which is beyond description, numbers of the most gloriously coloured birds, fishes of the most marvellous shapes & colours and, in short, a year's examination would hardly suffice to make one acquainted with all the beauties of this most unique & superb museum.

From the ceiling are suspended a number of lamps of different kinds, and curiously coloured, which give one a faint idea of what the Chinese feast of lamps must be. When you take into consideration the extraordinary mass of rare & beautiful objects collected together in this hall, their immense intrinsic value (independently of their worth as curiosities), it must be admitted that a more magnificent and valuable donation has never been made by an individual to any city in the world, & the Philadelphians have good reason to be proud both of their museum and its donor.

I could hardly tear myself away from such a scene of enchantment & it was not til' I got into the street that I found it was close to 2 o'clock, at which time the train for New York was to start, and I hurried back to the mansion house to prepare for the journey. I regretted much not having time to see the Waterworks, which are the finest in the world of their kind, but I could not spare another day.

We left Philadelphia about 1/2 past 2, and after a pleasant journey of 5 hours, arrived at New York. The country is quite flat & although highly cultivated, is not very interesting. We passed thro the small towns of Burlington, Bordentown, and Amboy, at which latter place we embarked on board a ferry steamer to cross to Staten Island, at the east side of which we entered another ferry boat, which took us to the quays of New York. It was too late to see anything of the City when we arrived, so we had a diner a L'Anglaise with Warre & Vansittart, whom we found on our arrival at the Globe Hotel in Broadway. Here we found numbers of acquaintances, among whom I was glad to meet Preston of the 7th Hussars, and during the whole evening we were [so] pestered with inquiries about Buffalo that we began to dread the very mention of them.

[18th]. I should say New York was about the size of Birmingham. The streets are not nearly so clean nor the houses so handsome as at Philadelphia, but the generality of the shops are good and it strikes one on the whole as a fine city. Broadway is the principal street being, I think, 2 miles long, but in breadth it is not superior to New Bond St. which it very much resembles. We drove down to the quays to look at the Bay & shipping, and went on board the Great Western & British Queen.

The view from the Battery, a public walk at the South end of Broadway on the border of the water, is very beautiful.

Opposite to it are the heights of Jersey, crowned with handsome buildings and about 1½ mile across the Bay, while the Bay itself is covered with craft of all descriptions, among which the beautiful Havre & Liverpool packets are conspicuous. We strolled about the town most of the day, and in the evening all dined together. Preston and I agreed to go to Canada together by the afternoon steamer tomorrow. Windham & Warre went up by the morning boat this day, and Greenwood having resolved to accompany Denny & Crawford to England, our party was now completely broken up after having travelled together nearly 5,000 miles. Some of us went to the theatre this evening, where we saw Fra Diavolo got up in capital style, and a very good comedy afterwards.

[19th]. The only sight I had time to go to today was Wilson & Anderson's collection of birds, which is very beautiful. There are upwards of 500 drawings of birds the full size of life & most beautifully executed, and they comprise nearly all the species belonging to North America (Since then it has been sold by auction & dispersed, to the disgrace of the New York people, for not securing such a monument of native or naturalized genius).

During the rest of the day I was engaged in packing & other business, but in point of fact there is very little to see in New York except the natural beauties of the environs, in which few cities are richer. Preston & I dined together at 3 o'clock, and at 1/2 past 5 embarked on board the steamer going up to Albany, among upwards of 700 other passengers. The weather began now to feel wintry and as the evening came on we were glad to retreat below, out of the chilling & frosty air.

The passengers were all at tea at 2 ranges of tables laid on each side of the cabin, nearly the whole length of the steamer. We looked for a moment at the scene of destruction and then returned to the deck, where getting into the engine room we remained smoking for about 1/2 an hour. We then went down to the cabin again, but what a change! In that short space of time the whole cabin had been completely filled up with standing bedplaces so that there was only just room to walk up the middle & sides. This transformation is effected by means of the tables, which in these boats, so liable to be overcrowded, are made to change into bedsteads containing 2 tiers of beds, and in a couple of hours they, as well as the double tier of side berths on each side, were filled with snoring (& spitting) occupants. I had taken up a very comfortable position in one of the side berths, & Preston in the one below me, but just as we were getting into our just sleep we were turned out by the real owners, having mistaken our ticket numbers.

We could not be at the trouble of going to bed again and went on deck. About 1 in the morning a loud crash proclaimed that something had gone wrong and presently we stopped & found that the cylinder had broken.

Every body turned out of bed, men, women & children, and such a babel of tongues I never heard. The deck was so slippery from a little rain having fallen in the evening, followed by a hard frost, that wherever you turned somebody was sprawling at full length, & the people were rushing about looking for luggage &c. In short I never beheld such a scene of confusion in my life. Preston & I had got into a comfortable corner with all our baggage around, us and we were highly amused.

Presently another steamer was heard coming up and we were then informed by 2 or 3 niggers who walked about ringing handbells, that the whole 700 of us were to be transferred to this new comer, she already having 500 passengers on board of her. Then ensued a scene of running, screaming, cursing, stumbling and misere, which may be imagined but not described. Wretched half-dressed maids & children rolling about the crowded decks, carrying their clothes and baggage about from place to place, amid the stream of people rushing towards the plank at the stern by which we were to gain the other boat, dogs barking & yelling in the dense throng, the sailors (!!!) roaring & bawling themselves hoarse, while the stunning noise of the two steamers letting off their steam at the same time, and the splashing & surging of the water, formed a din of sounds that was perfectly bewildering.

However, in about an hour the whole business was over & we were once more on our way to Albany. Preston & I got into a pile of carpet bags, where we contrived to get a shivery sort of sleep for an hour or two.

[20th]. At 6 this morning we ran alongside the wharf at Albany, a very fine town which rises off the right shore of the Hudson, about 120 miles above New York. As the railway train for Saratoga was to start at 8 o'clock, we had our luggage taken up to the office at once, & got some breakfast at an Hotel near it. The morning was so bitterly cold that I was very glad to be able to purchase a very handsome Buffalo robe, my dress not being well calculated for winter.

We started at 8 punctually on a very good railroad which goes thro Schenectady and Ballston to Saratoga. The country is pretty, the road being mostly in the valley of the Mohawk, in which the small town of Schenectady is built. As you approach Saratoga, you begin to distinguish the wood-clad mountains which surround Lake George (the Horican of Cooper's Last of the Mohicans) and form one of the most beautiful Alpine districts in America. The situation of Saratoga itself must, in summer, be very pretty, but I never was in a more deserted, wretched looking place than it seems in Winter. It is a village of immense Hotels and during the summer and Autumn it is thronged with people of every caste from all parts of the States who go there partly for the benefit of the celebrated mineral springs, and partly for fashion, and there, about September, you may meet the elite of all the rank, beauty, wealth, & talent of America.

However in a cold frosty day in Nov/r we were very glad to see as little of it as possible, and accordingly, having with a great deal of trouble succeeded in getting a waggon & pair, we proceeded on our journey about 3 o'clock, and after passing thro a most lovely country forming the outskirts of the Lake George Mountains & in which hill & valley, rich woods & bright streams, combine to form a most enchanting landscape, we arrived at the village of Sandyhill, where we dined and got beds. We here learned that the last steamer for the season was to leave Whitehall for St. Johns tomorrow afternoon, and we were not without misgivings as to whether, in the then state of the roads we should be in time to save ourselves a land journey of 150 miles at the worst of all seasons and over the worst of all possible roads.

[21st]. At one o'clock this morning (oh! what a wretched cold morning it was!) our Jehu roused us out of our beds, and without wasting much time on our toilet, we got into the sleigh (which it was considered advisable to take in preference to a waggon) and started. For the first 5 hours we travelled in darkness, and not above 3½ miles an hour, for there was no snow or ice on the roads in many parts & very little in any, and it is impossible to conceive more severe work for horses than dragging a sleigh under such circumstances. When we could see, the country around us was not in any way remarkable & we went alongside the Whitehall & Albany, or Champlain canal a great part of the way, and about 1 o'clock had the pleasure of perceiving the bluffs of Whitehall, and oh joy of joys! the white masts of the steamer peering above some of the houses.

In ten minutes more we were at the door of the Hotel where we were astonished to find Windham, Warre & 2 Guardsmen who had accompanied them from New York (one of whom was young Oswald) so that although they had started a day before us, they had gained nothing by their haste. We all dined together at the Hotel, and at 5 o'clock the Burlington Steamer, the finest on all the North American waters, bore us away from Whitehall. And at 7 o'clock next morning I had the pleasure of walking into my own room in St. Johns Barracks, having since I left it travelled upwards of 5000 miles.

W.F.

Journal of an Expedition
to the
Grand Prairies
of the
Missouri,
1840,

Bibliography

Articles

"Buffalo Hunting in the Far West." *American Turf Register and Sporting Magazine* XIV (May 1843): 249-51, Louisville.

Beers, Henry P. "Military Protection on the Santa Fe Trail to 1843." *New Mexico Historical Review* XII:2, April (1937): 127, Albuquerque.

Crease, Craig. "The Lone Elm and Elm Grove Case: a Study in Mistaken Identity." *Overland Journal* 11:1, Spring (1993): 24-31. Oregon California Trails Association, Independence.

The Gentleman's Magazine, XXIV (London, December 1845) report of recent deaths.

Gilbert, Bil. "Thar Was Old Grit in Him." *Sports Illustrated* 58:2 (17 January 1983): 58-72, Los Angeles: Time, Inc.

Holmberg, James J. "I Wish You to See & Know All; the Recently Discovered Letters Of William Clark to Jonathan Clark." *We Proceeded On* 18:4, November (1992): 4-12. Lewis and Clark Heritage Trail Foundation, Inc., Louisville.

Hummel, Nathan. "Nathan Dunn." *Quaker History,* Spring (1970): 34-39. Friends Historical Association, Philadelphia.

Kaufman, Kenneth C. "The Artist as Historian: George Catlin and Karl Bodmer Among the Mandan Indians." *Gateway Heritage* 10:1 (Summer 1989): 18-33. St. Louis: Missouri Historical Society.

Sunder, John E. "British Army Officers on the Santa Fe Trail." *Missouri Historical Society Bulletin* 23 (January 1967): 147-57. St. Louis: Missouri Historical Society.

Thurman, Melburn D. "Lone Elm Kansas: the History of a Trail Campground." *Overland Journal* 4:4 (1986). Oregon California Trails Association, Independence.

BOOKS

Eighteenth Biennial Report of the Board of Directors of the Kansas State Historical Society. Topeka: State Printing Office, 1913.

The National Cyclopaedia of American Biography, 306-7. New York: James T. White & Co., 1900.

The Journal of American History. Associated Publishers of American Records, n.d.

Appleton's Cyclopaedia of American Biography. Edited by James Grant Wilson, and Fiske, 673-4. New York: D. Appleton & Co., 1898.

Audubon, Maria A. *Audubon and His Journals.* New York: Charles Scribner's Sons, 1897, two volumes.

Barry, Louise. *The Beginning of the West.* Topeka: Kansas State Historical Society, 1972.

Betts, Robert B. *In Search of York.* Boulder: Colorado Associated University Press, 1985.

Buckingham, J. S. *The Eastern and Western States of America.* London: Fisher, Son & Co., 1842.

Burke, Bernard and Burke, Ashworth. *A Genealogical and Heraldic History of the Landed Gentry of Great Britain.* London: Harrison & Sons, 1906.

Burke, Bernard. *Burke's Genealogical and Heraldic History of the Peerage, Baronetage and Knightage,* 104. Edited by Peter Townsend. London, 1967.

Burke. *Burke's Genealogical and Heraldic History of the Landed Gentry.* Edited by Pirie-Gordon. London, 1939.

Chicester, Henry and Burges-Short, George. *The Records and Badges of Every Regiment and Corps in the British Army.* facsimile edition of Gale and Polden, Ltd. edition (London, 1900) London: Frederick Muller, Ltd., 1970, microfilm.

Duffus, R. L. *The Santa Fe Trail.* New York: The Tudor Press, 1936.

Ewers, John C. *Artists of the old West.* New York: Doubleday & Co., 1965.

_________, and et al. *Views of a Vanishing Frontier.* Omaha: Center for Western Studies/Joslyn Art Museum, 1984.

Field, Matthew. *Prairie and Mountain Sketches. In The American Exploration and Travel Series.* Edited by Kate L. Gregg and John Francis McDermott. Norman: University of Oklahoma Press, 1957.

Fortescue, J. W. *A History of the British Army.* London: MacMillan and Co. Limited, 1923.

Franzwa, Gregory M. *Maps of the Santa Fe Trail.* St. Louis: The Patrice Press, 1989.

Gregg, Josiah. *Commerce of the Prairies.* Edited by Max L. Moorhead. Norman: University of Oklahoma Press, 1954.

Hamilton, F. W. *The Origin and History of the First or Grenadier Guards.* London: n . p., 1874 .

Harris, Edward. *Up the Missouri with Audubon: the Joumal of Edward Harris.* Edited by John Francis McDermott. Norman: University of Oklahoma Press, 1951.

Johnston, William R., and et al. *Alfred Jacob Miller: Artist on the Oregon Trail.* Edited by Ron Tyler. Fort Worth: Amon Carter Museum, 1982.

Kelso, J, and J.H. Rutherfurd. *Rutherfurd's the Southern Counties Register & Directory.* Selkirk, Scotland: Borders Regional Library 1990, re-issue of 1866 edition published in Edinburgh.

Ketton-Cremer, R. W. *Felbrigg.* London: Rupert Hart-Davis, 1962.

Maximilian, Prince of Wied. *People of the First Man.* Edited by David Thomas and Karin Ronnefeldt. New York: E.P. Dutton & Co., 1976.

______. *Travels in the Interior of North America.* Three volumes of *Early Western Travels: 1748-1846.* Edited by Reuben Gold Thwaites. Translated by Hannibal Evans Lloyd. Cleveland: The Arthur H. Clark Company, 1905, 1906.

MeDermott, John Francis, and et al. *Travelers on the Western Frontier.* Edited by John Francis McDermott. Urbana: University of Illinois Press, 1970.

Merritt, John L. *Baronets and Buffalo.* Missoula MT: Mountain Press Publishing Company, 1985.

Porter, Mae Reed, and Odessa Davenport. *Scotsman in Buckskin.* New York: Hastings House, Publishers, 1963.

Riddle, Kenyon. *Maps of the Santa Fe Trail.* Raton, NM: Raton Daily Range, 1949.

Ross, Marvin C. *The West of Alfred Jacob Miller (1837).* Norman: University of Oklahoma Press, 1951.

Simmons, Marc. *Following the Santa Fe Trail: a Guide for Modern Travelers.* Santa Fe: Ancient City Press, 1986.

Sprague, Marshall. *A Gallery of Dudes.* Boston: Little Brown and Co., 1967.

Stewart, William Drummond. *Edward Warren.* Missoula: Mountain Press Publishing Company, 1986.

Tykal, Jack B. *Etienne Provost: Man of the Mountains.* Liberty, UT: Eagle's View Publishing Company, 1989.

Walford, Edward. *The County Families of the United Kingdom.* London: Robert Hardwicke, 1865.

_______. *Walford's County Families of the United Kingdom.* London: Spottiswoode Co. Ltd.7 1906.

Warner, Robert Combs. *The Fort Laramie of Alfred Jacob Miller.* Laramie: University of Wyoming, 1979.

Warre, H[enry] J[ames]. *Overland to Oregon in 1845: Impressions of a Journey Across North America.* Edited by Madeleine Major Frégeau. Ottawa: National Archives of Canada, 1976.

Wilhelm, Paul, Duke of Wurttemberg. *Travels in North America 1822-1824.* Edited by Savoie Lottinville. Norman: University of Oklahoma Press, 1973.

Windham, Sir Charles Ashe. *The Crimean Diaries and Letters of Lieut-General Sir Charles Ashe Windham KCP.* Edited by Maj. Hugh Pearse. London: Kegan, Paul, Trench, Tubner Co., Ltd., 1897.

MANUSCRIPTS

Register of Births, Marriages, Deaths of Scotland 1720-1854. *In Family History Library, Church of Jesus Christ of Latter Day Saints.* Microfilm of original register, Salt Lake City.

Register of Deaths 1868, Lauder Parish, County Berwick. In *Family History Library. Church of Jesus Christ of Latter Day Saints.* Microfilm of original records, Salt Lake City.

Fairholme, William. *The Journal of an Expedition. 1840.* The Huntington Library, San Marino CA, 1843.

Hulbert, Archer Butler. "The American Transcontinental Trails." In *The Crown Collection of American Maps Series IV,* vol. 5. Santa Fe, n.d.

Pilcher, Joshua. letter to Major R. W. Cummins, Indian Agent, Westport. William Clark MSS, Kansas State Historical Society, Topeka, 25 August, 1840.

Warre, Henry James. *In Days of Peace and War.* National Archives of Canada, Ottawa, 1896, microfilm of proof copy with Warre's notes, comments.

NEWSPAPERS

The Times. London.

Daily Missouri Republican, 8/17, 11/10 1840. St. Louis.

Index

William Fairholme's *Journal of an Expedition to the Grand Prairies of the Missouri, 1840,*
by Jack. B. Tykal
has been printed in an edition of 750 copies.
Typesetting in Caslon Old Style by Barbara Soles.
Printed and bound by Braun-Brumfield, Inc.,
Ann Arbor, Michigan.
Designed by Robert Clark.